Something to
help you sleep.
Christmas 95.
L. P.

# FRIEND OR FOE

*By the same author:*

The Russian Convoys 1941–45: Arms and Armour Press, 1987
British Submarines of the Second World War: Arms and Armour Press, 1987
Die Royal Navy auf der Donau 1918–1925: Herbert Weishaupt Verlag, 1988
British Submarines of the First World War: Arms and Armour Press, 1990
The T-Class Submarine: Arms and Armour Press, 1990
Midget Submarines: Arms and Armour Press, 1990
Belsen 1945 – Eyewitness Accounts: Trustees of the Imperial War Museum,
1991
Arctic Victory: The Story of the Arctic Convoys 1941–45: Arms and Armour
Press, 1993

# FRIEND OR FOE

Friendly Fire at Sea
1939–1945

by

Paul Kemp

LEO COOPER
LONDON

First published in Great Britain in 1995 by
LEO COOPER
190 Shaftesbury Avenue, London WC2H 8JL
an imprint of
Pen & Sword Books Ltd,
47 Church Street,
Barnsley, South Yorkshire S70 2AS

A CIP record for this book is available from the British Library

ISBN 0 85052 385 0

Typeset by Phoenix Typesetting, Ilkley, West Yorkshire
Printed by Redwood Books Ltd, Trowbridge, Wilts.

# Contents

# Introduction & Acknowledgements

This book began after a conversation with a distinguished British submariner whose submarine was extensively damaged in an attack by a Fleet Air Arm Swordfish. A brief look through some basic reference works confirmed that the incidence of "friendly fire" during the Second World War was fairly widespread. To begin with, any author writing on this subject faces a problem of vocabulary. The terms used to describe incidents where both participants were from the same side are many and various: Self Inflicted Losses; Own Goals; Amicide; Fratricide; Blue on Blue; Americide (Anglicide?) and Friendly Fire; although as General H. Norman Schwarzkopf said following the Gulf War, "once a bullet leaves a muzzle or a rocket leaves an airplane, it is not friendly to anyone". None of these terms are very satisfactory, but I have chosen to stick with Friendly Fire. All these terms are light-hearted ways of describing incidents which are deeply tragic. It has become the fashion lately, particularly with the media treatment of certain recent events, to treat such incidents as bordering on the farcical. It is true that they are often attended by a certain black humour, but that must not disguise the fact that ships are sunk or damaged, people are killed and wounded, families are left desolate and the "perpetrators", for want of a better word, are often left with an overwhelming sense of guilt.

To the layman, the whole concept of Friendly Fire is difficult to understand. How is it possible, I've been asked, for British aircraft to sink two British ships off the French coast on a clear, sunny day? The sensitive nature of the subject gives rise to all sorts of conspiracy theories and strange stories. In a recent television documentary a former British submariner implied that the French submarine *La Perle* had "disappeared" and that foul play was responsible. In fact *La Perle* was sunk in error by the British aircraft (see pages 112–116). There are no guilty men in this book and no dark secrets. Mistakes happen in all forms of life and warfare is no exception. Friendly fire has been a factor in war since the first caveman went into action with a bunch of stones. If the phenomenon of friendly fire is to be understood it must be de-sensationalised

The incidents in this book cover all the participants in the Second World War and are arranged by type: aircraft vs submarine; ship vs ship. In each the victim is the last named. Any such survey is unlikely to be fully comprehensive and anyone reading this book with a knowledge or experience of the War at Sea may well know of other incidents. Research into this subject is complicated by the diffuseness of sources and non-availability of records, while the invariably sensitive nature of the material sometimes leads to it being ignored in the official record either by deliberate omission or because the participants agreed to say no more about it.

Incidents involving British, American, French, German and Italian forces are well documented, those involving Soviet or Japanese forces less so. Although Russian authorities have cooperated in the research for this book, only three incidents involving Soviet sources have come to light (and one of those was Anglo-Soviet). Official reluctance to admit that mistakes took place is certainly a factor, but the limited nature of Soviet naval operations in the Second World War is more likely.

With regard to Japan, not one single incident has come to light. It is easy to accept that the Imperial Japanese Navy was either lucky or that their staff work was of such quality that deconfliction was preserved at all levels. However, the Japanese also share a reluctance to commit the truth to paper. The saying *Haigun no sho hei o Katarazu* (defeated generals should not talk of battle) still holds good. The western historian is also frustrated by the Japanese concept of *Tatemae*: that which goes in the record is what the authorities consider the acceptable version. Doubtless there are some Japanese incidents but the details are hard to come by.

It gives me great pleasure to express my gratitude to those who have contributed material for this book, or who have allowed me to quote from their papers or correspondence: the late Admiral Sir Frederick Parham; Vice Admiral Sir Hugh Mackenzie; Vice Admiral Sir John Roxburgh; the late Rear Admiral Richard O'Kane; Rear Admiral Robert Welland; the late Captain John Stevens; Commander Arthur Pitt; the late Kapitän zur See (a. d) Peter Cremer; Commander J. Stewart Moore; Commander E. E. Barringer; John Price and Lieutenant Commander Vernon Smythe.

I am also deeply grateful to: Horst Bredow of the U-Boot Archive at Cuxhaven; J. D. Brown FRHistS and the staff of the Naval Historical Branch of the Ministry of Defence, especially Mike MacAloon; Fleet Admiral V. I. Chernavin, Chairman of the State Historical Commission of the Russian Federation; Dick Boyle for doing my picture research in America; Commander P. R. Compton-Hall of the Royal Navy Submarine Museum, who has generously allowed me unrestricted access to the unrivalled collections in his care; Dr Steven Finnigan of the Submarine Force Library and Museum in Groton, Connecticut; Tom Hartman for editing the manuscript; Brian Head for a few very useful pointers; Dr Peter Jung of the *Kriegsarchiv* in Vienna; David Lees; Jane Middleton for introducing me to the mysteries of Word6 for Windows; Dott. Achille Rastelli; Dr J. van Royen of the Institute for Maritime History of the Royal Netherlands Navy; James Rusbridger; Charles Stirling, David Webb and Michael Wilson.

Special thanks are due to the late Captain John Coote who many years ago, encouraged me to turn some very disorganized research into a book; to Gus Britton for his usual trenchant criticisms of the manuscript, and to my wife Kitty for her support during my long periods chained to the word processor.

All errors and omissions are my own.

Paul Kemp
Maidstone, June 1994.

# CHAPTER ONE

## *The Problem*

Have rammed and sunk enemy submarine. Survivors appear
to speak Italian.

*Commanding Officer of HMS* Cyclamen *on sinking the Italian
submarine* Guglielmotti *on 10 March, 1917*

Friendly fire has been a feature of warfare since the beginning of
time. In describing the battle of Epipolae between the Athenians
and Syracusans in 413 BC, the Greek historian Thucydides wrote:

> The Athenians now fell into great disorder and per-
> plexity. . . . seeking for one another, taking all in front
> of them for enemies even though they might be now
> some of their flying friends. They ended by coming into
> collision with each other in many parts of the field,
> friends with friends and citizens with citizens, and not
> only terrified one another, but even came to blows and
> could only be parted with difficulty.[1]

Over two thousand years later a historian writing for the house
journal of the United States Army War College after the 1991 Gulf
War came to the conclusion that:

> We must face the unpleasant reality that the total
> elimination of friendly fire casualties on the modern
> battlefield is not possible.[2]

However, in terms of naval warfare, it is a phenomenon which has
only really made its mark in the twentieth century. That is not to

1

say that there were no friendly fire incidents at sea before 1900, but since then the problem has become acute and exacerbated by the introduction of new weapons systems and technology.

In the days of the great sailing fleets recognition was not such a problem. During naval engagements everything happened so much more slowly, while gunnery ranges were fairly close. To begin with the speed of warships was so much slower. Surviving reports suggest that by the mid-eighteenth century maximum speeds of 12 or 13 knots were possible for the latest ships of the line. A frigate could make up to 15 knots. These were exceptional speeds and required the unusual combination of high wind, so that maximum canvas could be set, a low sea state, so that the ship would not be impeded by pitching, and the ship having a clean hull. A ship which had been at sea for some time would be very much slower.

In the age of sail the effective range of weapons could be measured in hundreds of yards. The 32 pdr, which was the largest regularly-used long gun, had an extreme range of 2900 yards with a single shot; 500 yards with double shot; 1450 yards with grape; 1150 yards with case shot and 800 yards with double-headed shot.[3] However, these ranges were theoretical. Although engagements usually began with an exchange of fire using long-range carronades, ships would close to point-blank range. The epic duel between the *Shannon* and the *Chesapeake* was conducted at a range of 40 yards. When the former Emperor Napoleon asked Captain Maitland of HMS *Bellerophon* whether HMS *Superb*, then sailing at a cable's distance (240 yards) away, was near enough for an engagement, Maitland replied:

> I answered that half the distance, or even less, would be much better; as it was a maxim in our navy not to be further from the enemy than to give room for working the yards and manoeuvring the ship.[4]

Short ranges meant that the guns could be fired with double shot, with the attendant disastrous effects on the hull and rigging. A secondary factor was that not every gun would have a trained gun captain capable of laying the weapon at maximum range. The target had to be close enough that, in the appalling din of the gun deck, the gunners could see the target, point their gun at her, knowing that the shot would strike home.

The whole tempo of naval warfare in the age of sail was much slower. Given that sailing ships, with their towering masts and acres of canvas, were visible from a good distance, there was plenty of time , literally, to observe "the cut of his jib" before deciding to engage or not. At the Battle of Trafalgar in 1805 the British fleet approached the French at a speed of less than five knots and the first shot was not fired until the fleets were just over a mile apart. At the Battle of Lissa in 1866 between the Austrians and the Italians, which was the most significant naval battle between the Napoleonic Wars and the First World War, fire was opened at a range of just under 1000 yards. If anything the tactics used at the Battle of Lissa represented a step back since both sides viewed the ram as their main weapon.

However, the end of the nineteenth and the early years of this century saw naval development dominated by a technological revolution. Steam had replaced sail; iron, later steel, had replaced wood in ship construction; breech loaders had replaced muzzle loaders and shells replaced solid shot. Wireless telegraphy allowed naval authorities to communicate with ships worldwide when previously despatches would have taken weeks in transit. Gun ranges increased dramatically. The 13. 5 inch gun fitted in HMS *Iron Duke* had a maximum range of 23,740 yards at 20° elevation, while the Mk. 1 15-inch gun fitted in the *Queen Elizabeth* class battleships and the largest gun to be used by the Grand Fleet during the First World War had a maximum range of 33,550 yards at 30° elevation. Ships were also going faster. The maximum speed of a Grand Fleet dreadnought was 21 to 24 knots – nearly double that of a sailing ship of the line and, moreover, a speed that was not dependent on the vagaries of the wind. Greater speed and gun range meant that engagements were fought at greater ranges. At Trafalgar the range on opening fire was just over a mile: at the Battle of Dogger Bank in 1915 the range was 25,000 yards – twelve and a half nautical miles. .

New ships and weapons were introduced which would complicate matters enormously. Torpedo boats, submarines, aircraft, mines and a host of other devices transformed naval warfare from a momentous slogging match between two opponents. In 1914 commanders would have to consider the threat from the sea, from above the sea (although the days of the bomber or torpedo-carrying aircraft were still to come, the German naval air service did use Zeppelins for reconnaissance) and from beneath the sea: what would now be described as a "multi-threat environment". The introduction of the submarine and aircraft caused particular problems. Both were small and had many features in common regardless of their nationality. There were those who foresaw the problems which lay ahead. At that time it was fashionable to consider employing submarines as part of the fleet for scouting purposes. In the Royal Navy's summer manoeuvres of 1913 submarines were used in this fashion, but it became clear to Commodore Roger Keyes, the Commodore in charge of the Royal Navy's Submarine Service, that there were numerous problems of recognition and communication to be resolved.[5]

During the First World War there were numerous instances of friendly fire which showed the problems posed by these new weapons. Most incidents involved submarines in one way or another, which was inevitable given the threat posed by this new instrument of war. The Battle of Heligoland Bight on 28 August, 1914, was a confused engagement with British battlecruisers, cruisers, destroyers and submarines all milling about in poor visibility in a relatively small area. In particular the British submarines had not been warned of the presence of Vice Admiral Beatty's Battle-Cruiser Fleet whose unexpected intervention, ". . . was most embarrassing and caused one or two of the submarines much anxiety. "[6]

One submarine to be caused "much anxiety" was *E-6* (Lieutenant Commander Cecil Talbot) which:

> on two occasions got very close to one of our light cruisers and only refrained from firing when he actually distinguished the red St George's cross in her ensign; until then it did not occur to him that she might be a friend. This shows how close she was and the probability of a successful attack had *E-6* fired. On the second

4

occasion *E-6* was manoeuvred to allow the light cruiser to pass on a parallel course within 300 yards in order to make certain of identifying her ensign. Lieutenant Commander Talbot could hardly be blamed had he attacked, because in this particular operation he was clearly given to understand that only certain vessels were to take part. I submit however, that his care, patience and good judgement were worthy of praise.[7]

Talbot certainly acted with considerable restraint. Had he been spotted by one of the cruisers his submarine would probably have been rammed without hestiation. The incident illustrates many of the aspects of friendly fire which will become depressingly familiar throughout this book: poor information about disposition of friendly forces coupled with problems of recognition.

On 21 February, 1915, the German submarine *U-22* torpedoed and sank *U-7*. *U-22* had sailed from Wilhelmshaven on 13 February, 1915, an inauspicious day if ever there was one. Her commanding officer, *Kapitän-Leutnant* Wilhelm Hoppe, had been assured that no other U-boats would be in his area. On 21 February he sighted a submarine in poor visibility but was not sure of its identity. To be on the safe side, the challenge was given twice but no reply was received. Speed was now of the essence so Hoppe dived and, after further periscope observation, fired one torpedo which was seen to explode. It was only after *U-22* had plucked one survivor from amid the oil and wreckage that they learned that they had sunk their flotilla mate *U-7 (Kapitän-Leutnant* Georg Koenig).

One other German U-boat was lost during the First World War in circumstances which point to a case of friendly fire. On 10 July, 1918, the American submarine *AL-2* (Lt P. F. Foster USN) was on patrol in the Bristol Channel when an object was sighted resembling a buoy. As the submarine altered course to investigate, she was violently shaken by an explosion close by. As the geyser subsided a submarine periscope was observed. *AL-2* turned to ram, but the periscope disappeared. For the next twenty minutes those in *AL-2* could hear submarine motors and one submarine using her oscillator to communicate with another.

5

In Foster's opinion two U-boats were on the scene: one which had suffered the explosion and the other which had signalled by oscillator. Two German U-boats were in the area at the time, *UB-65* and *UB-108*, neither of which returned from patrol. It is conceivable that one of these boats was attacking *AL-2*, fired a torpedo which missed, ran on and struck the other U-boat. Strange? Certainly, but then so are many of the incidents described in this book. An alternative explanation is that the submarine, either *UB-65* or *UB-108*, fired a torpedo fitted with a magnetic pistol which the Germans were experimenting with at the time and which detonated prematurely. Either way, the Germans lost one submarine on 10 July, 1918, to one of their own torpedoes.

The Royal Navy lost four submarines in home waters due to friendly fire. On 16 September, 1917, the submarine *G. 9* (Lt Cdr Byron Cary) was rammed and sunk by the destroyer HMS *Pasley* (Commander Arthur Ramsey). *G. 9* was on patrol in the North Sea and had been warned about a U-boat operating in her area. It appeared that *G. 9* mistook *Pasley*, which was escorting a convoy to Lerwick, for the U-boat and fired two torpedoes at her just after midnight on 16 September. One torpedo missed astern while the other struck the destroyer abreast her engine room but did not explode. Just how this mistake occurred is not clear for *Pasley* was displaying a white light half way up her foremast as a guide for the merchantmen in her charge. No U-boat would burn a white light at night in enemy waters. Moreover *G. 9* had been warned about *Pasley*'s convoy passing through her area.

Just after the torpedoes had been fired *G. 9* must have realized her mistake for she made the correct challenge using the brightest light on board which lit up the entire submarine. But it was too late. The submarine was only 100 yards from the *Pasley* and steaming across her bows from starboard to port while the destroyer was swinging to starboard and increasing speed to ram. *Pasley* struck *G. 9* abreast the conning tower and she sank very quickly leaving only one survivor, Stoker William Drake.

The next victim was *H. 5* commanded by Lieutenant A. W. Forbes RN. At the end of February, 1918, *H. 5* departed from Bantry Bay for a patrol in the southern Irish Sea. Nothing more was heard from the submarine and her crew of twenty-five. At 2030 on 2 March the steamer *Rutherglen* sighted a submarine in position 53°4'N, 4°40'W crossing her bows at considerable speed. *Rutherglen*'s Master identified the submarine as a U-boat and rammed her. Cries were heard and men were seen swimming in the water but none were picked up. Since no U-boats were operating in the area at the time, *Rutherglen*'s victim was almost certainly *H. 5*. One of those killed was Ensign E. F. Childs of the United States Navy, an American submariner who was on board *H. 5* for some war experience. He was one of the first American casualties of the Great War.

It is not clear whether *Rutherglen* had been warned that a British submarine was operational along her route. Certainly neither party made any attempt to identify themselves. The Admiralty were not desperately concerned about the incident for *Rutherglen*'s crew were told that they had sunk a U-boat and they received the usual reward. The deception went so far as to sanction the award of the Distinguished Service Cross to *Rutherglen*'s Master *pour encourager les autres*. The reason for this was that the Admiralty constantly exhorted merchant ship masters to attack U-boats at every opportunity: the news that a British submarine had been rammed might well make others cautious.

The introduction into service of airships and aircraft caused British submarines to carry a deck recognition mark painted on a wooden cover over the fore hatch. These marks were changed at regular intervals. On 12 March, 1918, HM Submarine *D. 3* was on anti-submarine patrol in the English Channel off Dieppe when she was sighted by the French airship AT-0. *D-3* attempted to identify herself using rocket signals but to the crew of the airship it appeared that the rockets were being fired at their vulnerable hydrogen filled balloon. Moreover, the rockets were not the recognized inter-allied recognition signal. Accordingly they returned fire with a machine gun and the submarine dived. The airship crew immediately (and reasonably) assumed that the submarine was German and dropped six 52 kilogram depth bombs. Amid the explosions *D. 3* came to the surface briefly before sinking back into the depths. Four survivors were left swimming in the water, one of whom is said to have yelled to the airship crew as they hovered overhead, "You got us!", (the true response was probably a good deal stronger) whereupon Lieutenant Saint Remy, AT-0's com-

7

mander, realized that they might be British. Sadly he could not pick them up and, while he was searching for a ship to rescue them, the men drowned. The incident shows the real mess that allies could get into over recognition signals. The French airship did not use any and those fired by *D. 3* were not recognized as valid by the French. Moreover, the French did not see the deck recognition mark, a white circle on a black background, painted on *D. 3's* fore hatch.

The last British submarine to be sunk by friendly fire in the First World War was *J. 6* under the command of Lieutenant Commander Geoffrey Warburton RN. On 15 October, 1918, the Q-Ship *Cymric* was on patrol in the North Sea between the Firth of Forth and Blyth where a U-boat had been reported. It was a busy day for *Cymric's* crew, for two submarines had already been sighted but identified as friendly. Just after 1600 a third submarine was sighted which was identified as an enemy boat. One of the factors in the decision was that the submarine had a large white "U" painted on her conning tower. The ensign flown by the submarine could not be made out, but *Cymric's* commanding officer would not have been influenced by whatever ensign the boat was flying as he had once been deceived by a U-boat masquerading under the White Ensign. In any case the White Ensign and the war ensign of the Imperial German Navy looked remarkably similar when viewed from a distance.

The 4-inch guns of the *Cymric* had been tracking the submarine and, when the order to open fire was given, the submarine was engaged at point-blank range. The very first shell was on target. Meanwhile men on the submarine were trying to make a recognition signal. An officer trying to fire a rifle grenade was killed while another emerged from the fore hatch waving a white table cloth. *Cymric* ceased fire, but when the submarine altered course and headed for a fog bank, *Cymric's* captain believed he was being fooled again, so headed after her and continued to fire until the submarine was lost to sight in the fog.

*Cymric* went after her into the fog and was rewarded when the fog lifted and the submarine was seen ahead in a sinking condition. Only a small part of the conning tower was visible, while the bows were well out of the water. Some of the crew had boarded a small collapsible boat while others floundered in the water. When the collapsible drew alongside the Q-Ship, it was noticed that all the men wore cap tallies inscribed HM Submarines. Rescue work now began with a will with many of *Cymric*'s crew diving into the icy water to support the survivors until they could be rescued. Sadly only fifteen survivors of the submarine's crew of forty-four could be saved.

The submarine was *J. 6* which had identified the *Cymric* as a German vessel, which is not surprising given that *Cymric* was disguised to allay the suspicions of the most hard-bitten U-boat commander. The U on *J. 6*'s conning tower was made up of something hanging down from the conning tower and completing the loop of the "J". This was a case of mutual misidentification, but it was asking for trouble to have a Q-Ship and a submarine operational in the same area.

The Adriatic theatre, though not central to the conduct of the war, provided many interesting examples of how complicated the naval battlefield was becoming. In an effort to blockade the Austrian and German U-boats operating from ports on the Dalmatian coast, an Anglo-French-Italian force was established at Brindisi consisting of cruisers, destroyers, patrol craft, submarines and aircraft. To the normal difficulties of recognition were added the multiplicity of types of allied craft and all the difficulties of command and communication when the staffs were working in three different languages. There were numerous incidences of identification failures but two will suffice.

At all times a submarine patrol was maintained off the Austrian port of Cattaro (now Kotor). During the day this was a dived patrol with the boats deployed close inshore. At night the boats retired seaward to surface and recharge their batteries. Each submarine was allocated an area out of which she was not supposed to move. On the night of 17 April, 1918, the British *H. 1* (Lieutenant John Owen) sighted another submarine in her area.

According to the proceedings of the subsequent Board of Enquiry:

> The Captain of *H. 1* sighted at 7.45pm a submarine on the surface. He supposed that it was an enemy submarine as no allied submarine ought to have been in the

9

place where he supposed himself to be. He asked his navigating officer, Lieutenant Hayes, to look through the periscope and say whether it was an H class submarine. The navigating officer replied that it certainly was an enemy submarine. The Captain said that it looked very much like a UB type which has a flush upper deck and no raised forecastle. Lieutenant Owen continued to attack and fired two torpedoes one of which hit the submarine on the port side.[8]

Owen and his navigator were wrong. The submarine was the Italian *H. 5,* hopelessly out of position and virtually in the middle of *H. 1's* area. Moreover, she had surfaced before sunset, contrary to operational practice. In so doing, according to Commodore Howard Kelly, the British commodore at Brindisi, she was "looking for trouble"[9] There were only four survivors. The subsequent enquiry absolved *H. 1* of any blame, but it was decided that in future the practice of sending British, French and Italian boats to sea together would cease. Henceforth the submarines of one nation only would provide the patrol at any one time.

A side issue here is the difficulty of identifying a target through the periscope. The optics in the periscopes at the time of the Great War were fairly elementary. Periscopes were often subject to fogging particularly in warm climates. No clearer example of the difficulty of identifying a target through the periscope is offered than the experiences of the British submarine *H. 4* in the Adriatic on 28 September, 1916. In clear visibility she sighted what her commanding officer, Lieutenant Hugh Smyth, identified as a U-boat. Half an hour later Smyth fired two torpedoes at the "U-boat":

> These hit the point of aim immediately which was then identified as the branches of a tree which had the appearance of a submarine bridge.[10]

This incident must have led to some major leg-pulling back in the depot ship, not to mention Smyth having to explain why he wasted two torpedoes on a tree! However, it does show the difficulty of accurate periscope observation. A more amusing incident, but nevertheless one which could have had serious consequences, took place three months later. On 14 July, 1918, the crew of the French submarine *Artemis*, on patrol in the southern Adriatic, were hoping to enjoy some celebration of their national day. Alas it was not to be, for in the morning they were bombed by an Italian aircraft and in the afternoon hunted for three hours and given a good depth-charging by British destroyers.

Across the other side of the Peninsula an Italian submarine was lost because of the failure of the various port commands to keep up to date on shipping movements. On 10 March, 1917, the British sloop *Cyclamen* rammed and sank the Italian submarine *Guglielmotti* off the island of Capraia in the Tyrrhenian Sea. *Guglielmotti* was a new submarine and was proceeding from La Spezia to La Maddalena in Sardinia for trials. While en route she crossed the path of a southbound convoy escorted by *Cyclamen* who had been warned about U-boats in the area. When the darkened shape of the submarine was seen crossing the sloop's bows from port to starboard, she was immediately identified as a U-boat and rammed. It was only when the survivors were rescued that the mistake was realized. *Cyclamen* promptly made the signal which has achieved notoriety as an example of the black humour which so often attends these incidents:

> Have rammed and sunk enemy submarine. Survivors appear to speak Italian.[11]

The Italians were not amused, especially as fourteen of the submarine's crew had perished. The Italians had informed the French that the submarine would be crossing the route used by convoys, but were less impressed when they found that, despite the fact that the convoy had called at Porto Vecchio in Corsica, the French authorities had not warned those at La Maddalena that the convoy was heading south. A classic case of the left hand not knowing what the right was doing.

The waters around Britain were another area where the ships of three navies (Britain, France and the United States) were operating. The establishment of an American destroyer base at Queenstown in Ireland brought American forces into the same waters in which British submarines were operating. Both were engaged to the same purpose – the destruction of U-boats but it was inevitable that there would be errors in identification. On 29 February, 1918, the British submarine *L. 2* (Lt Cdr B. Acworth RN) was sighted by the American destroyers *Paulding, Davis* and *Trippe*. Despite giving the recognition signal, she was taken for a U-boat and fired on. Acworth dived the submarine only to receive a severe depth-charge attack which forced *L. 2* to a depth of over 300 feet[12] before coming to the surface. Once again she was fired on and a 3-inch shell went through the after end of the conning tower without exploding before Acworth's signalman could convince his assailants of his identity. Across the other side of the Atlantic the US Navy submarine chaser *SC-209* was less fortunate. On 27 August, 1918, she was taken for a submarine by the armed steamer *Felix Taussig* and sunk by gunfire.

Aircraft and submarines made the naval battlefield so much more complicated. In 1918 Admiral Sir Frederick Parham was serving as a sub-lieutenant in the patrol boat *P. 25,* a craft which, with its low silhouette, bore an uncanny resemblance to a submarine. During a two-month period in 1918 Parham endured the full gamut of friendly fire from airships, destroyers and merchant ships:

> We were bombed by a blimp at daylight, enthusiastically fired on by a US destroyer at dawn and deliberately rammed by a troop transport in the middle of a rainy middle watch. The bombs were few, small and missed. The American gunnery failed to register and was arrested by liberal use of a 10-inch signal lamp and some phrases which the Yeoman did not learn at the Signal School . . . In the encounter with the transport *P. 25* was split to the waterline but returned safely to port. All three of these aggressors were convinced that they were attacking a U-boat.[13]

Thus in the First World War the submarine and the aircraft posed considerable problems in terms of identification and recognition. In the inter-war period, the naval staffs of the various powers sought to learn from these mistakes and see how they could be prevented. The means and mechanisms established are the subject of the next chapter.

# CHAPTER TWO

## *The Search for a Solution*

There is no excuse for lack of vigilance. A good look-out is the
difference between life and death.

*Vice Admiral Max Horton, head of the Royal Navy's
Submarine Service 1940-1942.*

In essence friendly fire is caused by the failure to recognize friendly
forces on the battlefield. On the reasonable assumption that one
does not fire at one's own side deliberately, the causes for friendly
fire can be ascribed to failure of recognition. However, this goes
much further than a simple failure of mistaking "Brown for
Braun". The factors embraced by failure of recognition are many
and various and particularly so when considering the war at sea.

Ship recognition per se is a very difficult art. It is difficult for
those at sea but far more difficult for aircrew, particularly land-
based aircrew unfamiliar with the maritime environment. It is
made more difficult by numerous other factors: weather and light
conditions, failures of navigation, communications, Intelligence,
family resemblances between the same ships on different sides or
similarities in silhouette. Friendly submarines have been identified as surface ships. It is worth noting that the traditional and
legitimate use of disguises, false colours and decoys has sometimes
been a two-edged weapon.

Aircraft recognition is even more difficult and compounded by
the greater speed and smaller size of the aircraft. Aircraft are also
more difficult to spot, particularly when coming out of the sun.
Psychological factors such as stress caused by continual air attacks

and the absence of friendly air cover can lead to a lack of fire discipline which not only leads to friendly aircraft being fired on but also leads to safety arcs being ignored and fire directed at surface ships in company.

Communications and Intelligence failures are very common causes of friendly fire incidents. Factors here include the lack of knowledge of own forces' movements, the failure to communicate the details of own forces' movements to all authorities in an operational area, non-receipt of such communications and the failure to act on them. At unit level deficiencies in the communications and distribution arrangements at unit level may lead to the command and the weapons systems not having the same information. The Officer of the Watch might know that the aircraft in sight is friendly, but have all the gun positions been notified?

Errors in navigation are nothing new and may be caused by weather or equipment failure or human error. Navigational errors lead to ships and aircraft believing that they can attack targets at will, when, in fact, they are in a sanctuary or, on the other hand, believing that they are in a sanctuary when the reverse is true.

Recognition procedures exist to prevent friendly fire and must be adhered to. There have been numerous incidents due to the failure to give the correct challenge or reply or the failure to reply to a challenge. A particular problem here concerns submarines in a submarine sanctuary, an area where attacks on submarines are forbidden, when sighted by friendly aircraft. Does the submarine identify herself and hope that the aircraft is (a) in position and (b) aware of the sanctuary? Alternatively, should the submarine dive quietly out of way and pray that the aircraft will not take the dive as an "admission of guilt".

Recognition of friendly forces was assured by a number of means. To begin with there was training in the appearance and general characteristics of friendly ships and aircraft. This training would initially be carried out as part of a rating's general training and refreshed while at sea. Capital ships would sometimes have a compartment devoted to training in recognition where gunners and lookouts could be shown models or silhouettes of friendly and enemy aircraft under varying conditions of light. It was artificial but it was better than nothing.

In the Second World War British and American ships did not carry visible recognition markings when at sea. Their camouflage was designed to do the opposite: to make them blend into the prevailing sea and sky conditions as much as possible. Moreover, any aircraft sighted early in the war were probably Axis and it was felt that distinguishing marks would only serve to confirm the identity of a ship to an attacker. Safety lay in anonymity: an unmarked ship might be lucky and be ignored by the enemy.

On the other hand Axis ships did carry distinguishing recognition marks when in coastal waters where any aircraft sighted were more than likely to be friendly. German ships would carry the swastika emblem on the forecastle and quarterdeck and sometimes on top of gun turrets as well. However, when proceeding into the Atlantic on commerce raiding operations, these marks would be painted out. Any ship or aircraft encountered in the Atlantic would be hostile and there was no point in advertising the ship's identity. German U-boats in the Baltic belonging to one of the training flotillas wore bright distinguishing marks on their conning towers to prevent any misunderstandings. Italian ships wore bright coloured stripes painted on their forecastles early in the war. However, once the balance of air power was evened out in the Mediterranean, the recognition stripes disappeared.

The decision to wear recognition markings or not was finely balanced. Generally they were an advantage when ships were operating in areas dominated by their own air force. Recognition markings might have saved HMS *Britomart* and *Hussar* in August, 1944, from the fate which befell them at the hands of the RAF (see chapter eight). On the other hand recognition markings could be copied by the other side.

Visual recognition procedures were much the same among all the combatants in the Second World War. The systems described below relate to the Royal Navy but the procedures would have been identical in the US Navy, the *Regia Marina* or the *Kriegsmarine*. The challenge and reply system goes back to the earliest days of naval signalling. In Napoleonic times ships would identify themselves with combinations of numbered and lettered flags, while at night flares or lights hoisted on a special frame in the rigging would be used. It was the best way of confirming the identity of a ship.

The challenge and reply consisted of three-letter codes which did not make up a recognizable word. Thus TUK could be the challenge and BUX the reply. The message would usually be sent by directional signal light. For reasons of security purposes the challenge and reply codes were changed at regular intervals; every four hours was the practice in the Royal Navy. The codes were usually displayed somewhere prominent on the bridge or, in a submarine, in the control room. Some British signalmen in submarines were not above chalking the codes on the periscope standards for instant reference. British submarines were very proud of their skill at visual signalling (which was frequently abused to send messages of an inflammatory nature to other ships in company) and the qualified signalman (unique to British submarines: other nations employed combined telegraphists/signalmen) was seldom left in peace. The cry of "Signalman on the Bridge" was the call for everyone else in the boat to get out the way or flatten themselves against the bulkhead. Speed was of the essence in answering or giving a challenge and the signalman would not waste time on apologies if someone was flattened or sent flying in his rush to get to the bridge. Gus Britton was the signalman in the British submarine HMS *Uproar*:

> The call "Signalman on the Bridge" was regarded as an emergency call and anyone in the gangway made great haste to get out of the way. It took a few seconds to get to the control room, up the tower and on to the bridge. Often one of the lookouts had reached down into the tower and brought up the aldis lamp which had a red shade on it for night work.
>
> In 1945 when *Uproar* had returned from the Mediterranean, we were exercising round the back of Arran Island when I was called to the bridge at night. I was asleep on the wooden locker that had been my bed for two years and was on my feet and running while still asleep. The passage was dark with little light and in my

16

haste I tripped over a case which had been left in the passageway by a newly joined stupid ERA.[1] I sailed through the air and hit the steel lip of the coaming which secured the watertight door. I landed with the coaming just under my nose which was lucky . . . an inch lower and I would have lost all my teeth. The captain answered the signal while I was given a stiff tot and dumped on my locker. [2]

In enemy waters the signalman would have little or no signalling duties to perform, since submarine patrol areas were arranged so as not to conflict with surface ship operations. Any ships encountered could be assumed to be hostile. However, while on passage to or from patrol or in home waters, there would be unexpected meetings with aircraft or ships and, since submarines regarded themselves as vulnerable to the attentions of both sides, they would either dive or identify themselves until they had met their escort.

The challenge and reply system was not always foolproof and there were a number of encounters between ships of opposing sides which never came to anything because of confusion over the challenge/reply. In September, 1942, HMS *Tribune* was on patrol in the Arctic. Gus Britton was the signalman when the call "Signalman on the Bridge" came – as usual the call came in the middle of a meal:

A lookout had sighted a small dot on the horizon when we had crested a wave. I got up the 6-inch lamp, checked the challenge and reply and slowly made the challenge. After ten minutes of challenging the submarine, for that is what it surely was, made "AA" which is the international code for "What ship?" I repeated the challenge and he again made "AA". I challenged again and he made "AAA" which is international for "Plain language to follow". I told the captain that it was a U-boat but he did not believe me and said that it was one of our boats returning from screening a Russian convoy. I challenged him again and he made in English, "What name?" I challenged again and he made "What ship?" I

17

insisted as much as a signalman could that it was a U-
boat but the captain did not believe me. The submarine
then disappeared from sight.[3]

The U-boat had probably expended all her torpedoes and was
returning to port. Presumably the U-boat commander went away
muttering about incompetent signalmen and commanding
officers who didn't observe the regulations, and thinking of what
he was going to say to his flotilla commander about the matter on
his return from patrol

When dealing with aircraft, speed was of the essence in establishing identification. Ships carried coloured flares on the bridge,
or in submarines mounted on brackets on the periscope standards
or the side of the bridge. There were also 2.5 inch signal flares
which could be fired from a pistol. These were issued in a variety
of colours and were changed in the same way as the challenge/reply
codes. Early in the war rifle grenades were used to establish recognition but these were withdrawn after the loss of HMS *Oxley,* whose
grenades had failed to burst with tragic consequences and after a
French liaison officer on another submarine had managed to shoot
the signalman in the foot with one, causing mayhem on the bridge
while the grenade burned itself out On one occasion a British submarine was banned from carrying these pyrotechnics: when
aviation spirit was being carried to Malta in HMS *Rorqual's* external fuel tanks, the smell of kerosene was so strong on the bridge
that use of the recognition flares and grenades had to be banned.
However, given the general inability of RAF Coastal Command to
recognize such signals, their absence was not missed! While dived,
submarines could also fire a flare or coloured smoke candle through
an underwater gun set into the pressure hull in order to establish
identity with friendly surface forces.

Surface ships also carried fighting lights on their yardarms.
Fighting lights were usually red, green and white (the only practical colours at night when at sea) and could be used to establish
instant identity in a confused mêlée with enemy forces. They were
not used often as they were as much a point of aim for the opposition as they were an aid to one's own side. They could, however,
be very useful in a confused night action. However, visual means

18

of establishing identity were not foolproof. If details of such signals fell into the hands of the other side the challenge/reply could be used to deadly effect. In the night encounter on 31 May/1 June, 1916, which followed the Battle of Jutland the Germans made very effective use of British signals which they had intercepted.[4] As Admiral Sir John Jellicoe, Commander-in-Chief of the Grand Fleet, put it some days after the battle:

> When the destroyers challenged at night by flashing, the first flash (or certainly the second) told the Germans that the flashes were British and gave their exact position when as somebody put it, "On came the searchlights, off went the guns and down went the destroyer".[5]

The challenge/reply system could not replace visual identification.

The invention of radar required that means be found to identify contacts which were out of sight. This led to the development of IFF: Identification Friend or Foe. This was an automatic device which produced a coded echo when illuminated by a radar set. The contact could then be classified as friendly or hostile without having to resort to visual identification. The system promised much, particularly when used in conditions of poor visibility or when dealing with fast moving aircraft.

The problem of how to identify echoes seen on a radar display was one that had been addressed as early as 1938. Several methods had been tried but the one adopted was to fit a small transmiiter receiver, known as a transponder, in friendly aircraft. This received the signals from the locating radar and retransmitted them so that the amplitude of the echoes on the radar display increased perceptibly whenever the transponder made a reply, thus identifying the aircraft as friendly. But IFF had more uses than that. It could act as a navigational beacon or send a special signal indicating that the aircraft was in distress.

The Mk. I IFF responded only to the RAF's Chain Home air defence radar but the Mk. II followed almost immediately, responding to other air defence and ground radars as well as the Navy's Type 79 long-range air-warning set. It was subsequently modified to respond to the RAF's GCI (Mk. IIG) and the Navy's

Type 286, 290 and 291 air-warning radars. Mk. II IFF was crude and unreliable, but if the equipment worked, and if the aircraft remembered to switch it on, it did provide a limited answer to the recognition problem. MK. II was further developed when it went to sea as Type 252. Thus a ship fitted with Type 291 search radar should be able to identify a ship fitted with Type 252. There were worries that the enemy might be able to replicate the transponder but the risk was accepted.

However, the MK. II IFF suffered from the limitation that its IFF transponders could only respond to signals on a limited number of wavebands and there was a limit to the number of modifications the system could accept. The solution was the development of IFF Mk. III, a set which formed the basis for IFF systems used to this day. The Mk. III IFF was fundamentally different in that airborne and seaborne IFF transponders would no longer reply to primary radar signals but would respond to special "Interrogators". These were low-powered secondary sets fitted with the main set, so that their transmitted pulses were synchronized and the received signals displayed on the radar tube. As the main set swept over a contact, the interrogator would trigger a response from the transponder which would indicate the contact as friendly.

However, introducing IFF was easier said than done. It was decided to introduce Mk. III in one theatre at a time, but the task proved to be beyond the available resources. It proved impossible to ensure that all ships were changed over together, given operational commitments. The situation was worst in the Mediterranean where Mk. III was introduced at the time of the landings in Italy when the German air effort was on a considerable scale. The anti-aircraft cruiser *Delhi* reported that, while she was off Salerno, friendly aircraft displayed an astonishing variety of IFF including Mk. III, Mk. IIN, Mk. IIG, Mk. II, Mk. I or none at all.

IFF was useful but it had its limitations. There was a feeling that switching the set on might compromise a ship's position. Some commanders preferred to have it switched off. Too much reliance on IFF meant the possibility of a friendly ship being assessed as hostile (this happened) if their set was switched off or unserviceable. Moreover, there was the risk that the enemy would duplicate the transponder return and masquerade as "friendly". On 11 May, 1945, the aircraft carrier *Bunker Hill* was operating in support of American forces on Okinawa when she was hit by two Kamikazes which did immense damage. The Combat Air Patrol was up and all the carrier's radars were working, but somehow the two Japanese aircraft managed to penetrate the layered defences until they were right above the carrier. The action alarm was sounded the moment the first *Kamikaze* ploughed into *Bunker Hill's* flight deck. The Americans believed that the Japanese had succeeded either because their IFF could not cope with the number of friendly aircraft in the sky or, more likely, the Japanese were showing an early sign of their talent for electronics and were replicating the transponder transmissions from the Mk. III IFF. IFF was useful but it was not the hoped-for panacea.

Separation of friendly forces was another means of avoiding friendly fire. These restrictions were largely for the benefit of submarines who were most vulnerable to being wrongly identified. Submarines would be given patrol areas from which they were not allowed to stray, even when in pursuit of a target. In such circumstances they were to warn the boat in the next "billet" that a target was headed their way. The system worked but was vulnerable to errors of navigation whereby a submarine could stray into another's area by accident with disastrous consequences.

While en route to and from patrol submarines moved in a protected area, known as a Moving Haven. This was an area of ocean corresponding to the submarine's track in which attacks on submarines were forbidden. The position of the haven was adjusted each twenty-four hours to correspond to the submarine's progress. The system worked only if all commands were notified of the parameters of the haven. Its main disadvantage was that, given the unreliable state of aircraft navigation, an aircraft could be miles out of position and believe himself to be in an area where targets could be attacked at will when the reverse was the case. In waters near to ports used by submarines areas were permanently declared as Total Bombing Restriction areas or Submarine Sanctuaries. where all attacks on submarines were forbidden.

Visual recognition skills, visual challenges, IFF and separation of friendly forces were means whereby naval commands sought to avoid friendly fire. By and large, considering the scale of naval warfare in the 1939-45 war, the provisions worked. The next ten chapters contain details of the incidents where, for one reason or another, the system failed.

# CHAPTER THREE

## *Ships vs Ships*

We fought a spirited action with two of our own destroyers.

*British MTB report after night action in the Adriatic.*

In incidents between ships of the same side, failure of recognition was the single greatest cause of friendly fire. . As we have seen, recognition training using ship models, silhouettes and photographs was carried out as part of general naval training and continually "refreshed" at sea. Nevertheless poor visibility or the confusion attending an engagement often resulted in ships being wrongly identified and then engaged as if they were the enemy. One such instance (among many) occurred on 4 October, 1943, when HMS *Grenville* (Lt Cdr Roger Hill RN) in company with the destroyers *Limbourne* (Senior Officer), *Wensleydale, Tanatside* and *Ulster* were engaged in a confused mêlée with German destroyers in the English Channel. *Grenville* was struck aft by German shell-fire, which started a large fire. Then with destroyers milling about all over the place:

> One of the "Hunts" opened fire on us with a four-barrelled Pom-Pom; the tracers were going in a steady stream just over the bridge. If the gunlayer lowered his sight ever so slightly we were all dead. I felt if I raised my hand it would be blown off.
>
> I put on the switch for the identification lights, but the circuit was shot through, the circuit for the fighting lights on the yardarm and they did not go on either.

The Chief Yeoman came to the rescue with the ten-inch signalling lamp, "*Grenville* here, cease fire," and at last all the firing stopped.[1]

The presence of friendly ships of allied nations, with all the inherent communication problems, often only served to complicate matters. In March, 1942, convoy PQ. 13, on its way to Russia, was attacked by a force of three German destroyers and in the poor visibility there was a mêlée in which it was difficult to tell friend from foe. HMS *Eclipse* sighted a warship, in fact the German destroyer *Z. 26,* bearing 020°, but refrained from opening fire mistaking her for the cruiser HMS *Trinidad.* One of the Soviet destroyers (*Gremyaschi* or *Sokrushitelny*) was quicker off the mark and opened fire immediately. *Eclipse* was still trying to work out whether or not the ship being shelled was friendly or not when HMS *Fury* suddenly appeared out of a squall dead ahead of *Eclipse* and fired several salvoes at her before recognition was assured. *Fury* then turned back to screen the damaged *Trinidad* which had been hit by one of her own torpedoes (see Chapter 11). Lieutenant Commander E. Mack, in command of the *Eclipse,* decided that the risk of accident was too great with so many ships tearing round in the snow squalls, so altered course to the west, "as there seemed altogether too many destroyers around the convoy".[2]

The classic corollary of these incidents is the failure to identify a ship as hostile. There is no more perfect example of this than the sinking of the German destroyer *Friedrich Eckholdt* during the Battle of the Barents Sea on 31 December, 1942. A German task force, consisting of the pocket battleship *Lutzow,* the heavy cruiser *Admiral Hipper* and six destroyers, one of which was the *Friedrich Eckholdt*, a 1934A type destroyer built in 1937 and mounting five 12. 7cm guns. The Germans attempted to attack convoy JW. 51A heading for Murmansk. In the course of a long and confused action, fought in atrocious weather, the vastly superior German force was held at bay by the convoy's escort until the cruiser covering force consisting of HMS *Sheffield* and HMS *Jamaica*, under the command of Rear Admiral Robert Burnett, arrived. Burnett's intervention at a critical moment caused the cruiser *Admiral Hipper* to break off the action. As *Hipper* turned away, so Burnett followed in order to keep up the pressure. At this crucial stage a snow-squall gave the *Hipper* some cover, just as two German destroyers appeared out of the snow in a position which was ideal for a torpedo attack on the British cruisers. *Jamaica* fired at the distant destroyer, *Richard Beitzen,* while *Sheffield* turned toward the nearer ship, *Friedrich Eckholdt.*

> At thirty-one knots [wrote Captain Clarke, *Sheffield*'s commanding officer] the range closed with remarkable rapidity. In one minute we felt fairly certain that the ship was no friend of ours. With the director gunner's finger on the trigger, we made the battle challenge. The reply, a triangle of white lights, was unrecongizable, and a salvo of six 6" shells was sent on its way at a range of 4,000 yards. The shells, at an almost horizontal trajectory, roared towards the point-blank target.
>
> It seemed that certainly half the salvo hit. I could see sparks of penetration, followed by the flame and smoke of detonation. Each successive salvo equally found its mark. On opening fire I had agreed with the Admiral that in the last resort I should try and ram the enemy, but it became clear in a matter of two minutes that such an extreme step would become unnecessary. As we swept down on the target she was disintegrating under our eye, and with a *coup de grâce* from our close-range weapons as we passed her at a few hundred yards, followed for good measure by a few salvoes from our after turrets, *Friedrich Eckholdt* was left, a horrible and smoking ruin, to sink astern.[3]

Marine "Doddie" Thorndyke was gunlayer of the S.2 4-inch mounting (ie; the second 4-inch mounting on *Sheffield's* starboard side) and recorded the hail of fire that *Sheffield* was able to pour into the stricken destroyer:

> I was ordered to slip my guns into local [control] and managed to get off eighteen rounds at blank range. I could see boats being lowered, and also men manning

the torpedoes, but our pom-poms took care of those. The shells were certainly passing right through these men. I could also see men jumping off the stern, and the skipper was silhouetted against the flames around his bridge. She drifted astern like a grand fireworks display[4].

The *Friedrich Eckholdt* had made the mistake of thinking that *Sheffield* was one of her own and paid the price accordingly, although it is difficult to see how *Sheffield* with her straight stem, slab-sided superstructure and twin funnels could have been mistaken for *Admiral Hipper* with her raked clipper bow, pagoda-like superstructure and single funnel. The consequences of *Eckholdt's* lookouts' failure underline the reason why ship recogntion skills were, and are, so important.

On 25 September, 1939, the submarine HMS *Spearfish* reported that she had been severely damaged in a depth-charge attack near the Horns Reef off the Jutland coast and was attempting to return home using Danish territorial waters as much as possible (thereby displaying a fine disregard for Danish neutrality). Subsequently her commanding officer, Lieutenant J. H. Eaden RN, signalled that the submarine was unable to dive and requested an escort. In response to this appeal, three Hudson aircraft from RAF Coastal Command were sent to give air cover while ships of the Sixth Destroyer Flotilla, *Eskimo* (Captain D6), *Somali, Mashona* and *Matabele,*were ordered to meet the submarine, covered by the Second Cruiser Squadron, HM Ships *Sheffield* and *Aurora.*

During the afternoon of 26 September *Matabele* was diverted to investigate two merchant ships and then rendezvous with the cruisers, while *Eskimo, Mashona* and *Somali* went on ahead to rendezvous with *Spearfish* which they did at 0400 on the 26th. Meanwhile *Matabele* had finished searching the two merchant ships but failed to make contact with the cruisers, so headed for the rest of her flotilla meeting *Spearfish.* At about 0600 *Eskimo's* lookouts sighted another warship apparently shadowing the little group at a range of two miles, later opening out to four miles. After a hurried check revealed that there were no other friendly ships in the area *Eskimo* hauled out, increased speed and fired starshell preparatory to opening fire. Fortunately the starshell illuminated the familiar shape of a Tribal class destroyer – HMS *Matabele* – before any serious damage was done.

Rear Admiral Destroyers Home Fleet (RA[D]) commented that although *Matabele* was correct in seeking to rejoin her flotilla her commanding officer should have either closed the other destroyers quickly and identified himself or stood off till dawn when he could be more easily seen and identified. His doing neither of these things nearly had more serious results. However, when the various reports reached the Commander in Chief Home Fleet, Admiral Sir Charles Forbes, he expressed his disapproval of the general organization of the operation. Forbes was not particularly concerned over the *Eskimo*/*Matabele* incident, although he concurred with RA(D)'s comments. Instead, he was critical of the decision to arrange the rendezvous between *Spearfish* and the destroyers at night off an enemy coast when recognition would be at its most difficult, especially as the rendezvous was ordered for 0400, the exact hour at which recognition signals changed. *Matabele*, *Eskimo* (and *Spearfish* too) escaped without damage or casualties.

In the confusion surrounding the evacuation of the British Expeditionary Force from France in 1940 there was an incident in which one ship was sunk and a large number of casualties suffered. On 28 May, 1940, the twin-screw minesweeper HMS *Lydd* sailed from Dunkirk at 2250 carrrying in excess of 400 British troops. Early next morning she came across the sinking destroyer HMS *Wakeful* which had been torpedoed by a German *Schnellboot*[5] and was sinking. By the light of an Aldis lamp the bow and stern of the destroyer could be seen afloat, with men clinging to them. Together with the minesweeper HMS *Gossamer*, the *Lydd* tried to rescue as many of the *Wakeful's* company as possible. *Lydd* had picked up around ten men from the water when the destroyer HMS *Grafton* arrived on the scene, also returning from La Panne with 800 men on board. *Gossamer* returned to Dover leaving *Grafton* and *Lydd* to carry on with the rescue work.

Also on the scene was the drifter *Comfort* which, together with the drifter *Nautilus,* had been en route to La Panne. *Comfort* picked up sixteen of *Wakeful's* crew, including her commanding officer, Commander R. L. Fisher RN. She then went alongside *Wakeful's* stern portion to rescue more men, but, finding that it had capsized,

27

went alongside *Grafton's* starboard side to warn her of the danger of *Schnellboote* in the area. It was at this juncture that the *U-62* (Kapitän-Leutnant Hans Michalowski) appeared on the scene and fired one torpedo which struck *Grafton's* port side and blew away her stern. A second explosion (cause unknown for *U-62* fired only one torpedo) wrecked *Grafton's* bridge killing her commanding officer, Commander G. E. C. Robinson RN, and three others. The torpedo explosion swamped the *Comfort* (some of her crew and *Wakeful's* survivors, including Commander Fisher, were washed overboard) so she cast off ,and circled round until within 50 yards of the *Grafton.*

In the darkness and confusion *Lydd* and *Grafton* mistook *Comfort* for a *Schnellboot* and opened a heavy and accurate fire upon her with 4-inch and Lewis guns. *Lydd* then turned in and rammed the drifter squarely amidships cutting her in half. Some of *Comfort's* crew attempted to jump on to the *Lydd* but were repelled with rifle fire, the minesweeper's crew thinking that they were boarders. Two determined men did manage to gain the minesweeper's deck and it was then discovered that the rammed vessel was the *Comfort.* Only five men were saved from the *Comfort* of which four were survivors from *Wakeful.* After this tragic incident *Lydd* set course for Ramsgate since *Grafton* was floating on an even keel and seemed able to look after herself (she was sunk later that day by HMS *Ivanhoe* after her troops and ship's company had been taken off). Commander Fisher was left swimming until 0515 when he was picked up by the SS *Hird.*[6]

On 23 October, 1941, at 2337A[7] the destroyer HMS Cossack (Captain E. Berthon DSC RN) was torpedoed by *U-563* (Kapitän-Leutnant Klaus Bargsten) while escorting convoy HG-75 home from Gibraltar. The torpedo struck on the port side forward and although *Cossack* was in no immediate danger of sinking, the destroyer HMS *Legion,* corvette HMS *Carnation* and the Free French sloop *Commandant Duboc* stood by to render assistance. Shortly afterwards in the darkness *Legion* obtained a radar contact and the order was given to illuminate it with the searchlight. An object resembling a submarine was sighted and fire was opened using the 2 pdr Pom Pom. However, on further examination, the "submarine" proved to be the *Commandant Duboc.* Fortunately she was just beyond the range of the 2 pdr and no damage was caused. In this case the confusion on board *Legion* is understandable: a U-boat had just torpedoed a destroyer; but the situation was not helped by the fact that *Commandant Duboc*, with her low freeboard and turtle-back stern did bear an uncanny resemblance to a submarine! (Wags among her crew complained that she behaved like one in anything but a flat calm.)

*Commandant Duboc* got away with nothing worse than some ruffled gallic feathers. One month later in the North Sea HMS *Garth* was not so lucky. On the night of 19/20 November, 1941, convoy FS-50 was steaming south down the East Coast and was just to the north of Hearty Knoll lightship. Activity by German *Schnellboote* was expected and the Hunt class destroyer *Garth* ( Lt Cdr E. H. Dyke RN)) was stationed some five miles ahead of the convoy, although unfortunately her radar was unserviceable.

Meanwhile, steering north was the destroyer HMS *Campbell* (Captain C. T. M. Pizey RN) with *MGB. 87* in company. *Campbell* was engaged in an anti-E-boat patrol and intended to keep to seaward of FS-50. From 2100 the "Headache"[8] team in *Campbell* began to report concentrations of *Schnellboote* in the area and it became clear that the Germans were after the convoy. The nearest British ship was believed to be about five to eight miles or so away when a ship appeared on *Campbell's* port bow at about six cables' range. Pizey and his signalmen identified her as a *Schnellboot*.

The target was immediately fired upon with close-range weapons and starshell. When the starshell revealed the outline of a Hunt class destroyer – HMS *Garth* – fire was checked and recognition signals exchanged. *Garth* had been taken by surprise by the attack. Her lookouts had not spotted *Campbell* or the MGB. Lieutenant Commander Dyke later said that he found it:

> difficult to fully appreciate the situation as tracer bullets were whistling past my head as I stood by the pelorus.[9]

*Garth* had responded with 2 pdr pom-pom and Oerlikon fire but had come off worst in the encounter. Two of her crew were dead and eight wounded. Moreover, a 40mm shell from *Campbell* had fractured a main steam pipe in her boiler room and she had to be towed back to Harwich.[10] Despite this incident *Campbell* and *MGB. 87* finished the night's work with an engagement with the Schnellboote in which two were sunk and a third had to be abandoned later. It was, however, not an entirely satisfactory rate of exchange, for, in addition to Garth's damage, three of the merchant ships in the convoy were sunk by *Schnellboote*.[11]

This was one of the first instances where signals intelligence played a part in a case of friendly fire. *Campbell's* commanding officer had his instincts that *Schnellboote* were in the area confirmed by the "Headache" team. When *Garth's* shadow appeared out of the darkness, those on *Campbell's* bridge saw what they expected to see, despite the difference in size between a 1200-ton destroyer and a *Schnellboot* weighing just under 100 tons.

A month later in the Indian Ocean there was an incident which almost defies explanation in which the Indian anti-submarine vessel, a hired yacht, *Prabhavati,* was shelled and sunk by the cruiser HMS *Glasgow* on 8 December, 1941. Intelligence reports had been received which indicated that a number of German merchant ships interned in the Portuguese colony of Goa, on the west coast of India, were planning to break out. There were also reports of a German U-boat operating in the area. Accordingly the Commander in Chief East Indies, Vice Admiral G. S. Arbuthnot, ordered the cruiser HMS *Glasgow* to investigate the reports and search the Laccadive Islands in case U-boats were using the islands as a supply base.

At the same time the *Prabhavati* was towing two barges through the area of *Glasgow's* search. At about 1830Z on 8 December *Prabhavati's* crew were having difficulties with the tow and had brought both barges alongside to adjust the wires. This task must have been all-engrossing, for none of her crew saw the *Glasgow* approach or saw the challenge issued by the cruiser. From *Glasgow's* bridge it was hard to identify the target in the gathering dusk. A challenge was issued but no reply received. While the challenge was sent again, it appeared to those on *Glasgow's* bridge that the barges alongside the *Prabhavati* were the U-boat they were looking for, that the Indian vessel had been captured and boarded, and that the U-boat was still alongside. The absence of any reply to *Glasgow's* challenge only served to confirm this view. Consequently

30

*Glasgow* opened fire with her main armament and a few rounds of 6-inch served to dispose of the *Prabhavati.* There were a number of casualties among her crew and Admiral Arbuthnot wrote to the Viceroy of India, Lord Linlithgow, to express his regrets for the incident.

The closely fought night actions off Guadalcanal provided the right circumstances for errors in identification. On the night of 8/9 August, 1942, the cruisers HMAS *Canberra* and USS *Chicago,* together with the American destroyers *Patterson* and *Bagley,* formed the Southern Covering Force operating off Guadalcanal and were deployed to prevent the Japanese running troops and supplies into the island by night, following the American landings on the island on 7 August. That night the Japanese 8th Fleet, consisting of five heavy and two light cruisers and commanded by Vice Admiral Gunichi Mikawa, sailed from Rabaul for a raid on the invasion transports. On the morning of 9 August Mikawa's ships entered the narrows between Savo Island and Guadalcanal, passing the two radar picket destroyers undetected, and surprised *Canberra* and her consorts.

The Japanese kept the two cruisers under observation for some time before launching torpedoes at 0145. The Japanese ships had passed out of sight before either of the two destroyers could take any action, and no sooner had lookouts in the *Canberra* seen the tracks of torpedoes pass down either side of the ship from ahead than she was raked with 5.5-inch gunfire which reduced her upper-works to a shambles, with ten officers and seventy-four ratings killed. The *Chicago* (Captain H. D. Bode USN) had headed after the Japanese ships, but failed to make contact despite firing four four-gun salvoes of star-shell. It was at this moment that *Chicago* was struck by a torpedo on the port bow. The resulting structural damage did not for a moment affect her fighting ability, for after the bow had been shored up, Captain Bone pressed on at 25 knots and engaged the Japanese destroyer *Yunagi* before returning to see what had happened to *Canberra.* On sighting the *Canberra,* which was blazing furiously, her lookouts also noted another ship standing by. Without thought of a challenge *Chicago* opened fire. The destroyer returned fire and the engagement between the two ships continued for some time before the other ship was identified as

31

*Patterson.* No damage was done to either vessel, although the incident stands as example of the potential for error in a confused night action and the need, therefore, for accurate and easily remembered recognition procedures. The engagement between the *Chicago* and the *Patterson* was the least of the United States Navy's worries that night: the Battle of Savo Island represented a major disaster for American arms. In addition to the loss of the *Canberra,* the Americans lost three cruisers, *Astoria, Quincy* and *Vincennes* together with the destroyer *Jarvis,* a total of 1450 officers and men killed.

The New Zealand trawler *Kiwi* was the "victim" of two incidents of mistaken identity during the Pacific Campaign. In January, 1943, the exact date is unknown, she was missed by two torpedoes fired by the American torpedo boat *PT-45.* The PT boat was one of many such craft deployed to stop the night reinforcement of the Japanese garrison of Guadalcanal. The *Kiwi* was mistaken for one such Japanese vessel. Fortunately other ships of the New Zealand Navy were in the area and were working the same communications nets as the American PT boats. What are coyly described as "voice recognition procedures" made the Americans aware of their mistake. Kiwi's second incident was less fortunate. On the night of 24 May, 1943, while on passage from Auckland to Noumea, she was damaged by gunfire from the American motor vessel *J. B. Weaver* and was forced to return to New Zealand for repairs.

When investigating the incident, the New Zealand Navy Board found that there were no challenge/reply procedures in force for merchant ships and minor war vessels. Given the understandable tendency of merchant ships to shoot first and ask questions later, the New Zealand Navy Board asked for the appropriate recognition procedures to be put in place as soon as possible especially as *Kiwi* and her sister ships would continue to be employed in the forward area.

IFF (Identification Friend or Foe) was meant to end uncertainty about the identity of a ship in bad weather or when the situation was confused. Friendly ships would show up as such on radar operators' PPIs (Plan Position Indicators, an early form of radar screen). When IFF first went to sea, too great a reliance was placed in its capabilities. Such a mistake almost ended the career of the American destroyer *Spence.* On the night of 2 November, 1943, during the Battle of Empress Augusta Bay in the Solomon Islands, *Spence* was the senior ship of DesDiv 46 wearing the broad pendant of Commander R. L. Austin USN. In the confused high-speed manoeuvring *Spence* collided with her sister ship USS *Thatcher* and was then hit in an oil fuel tank, resulting in salt water contamination of fuel. Austin was forced to drop out of line and relinquish tactical command of his division to Commander L. R. Lampman in *Thatcher*. An hour later she encountered the Japanese destroyer *Hatsukaze* (who had just lost her bow in collision with the cruiser *Myoko*) and engaged her. At the same time *Spence* came under fire from four American destroyers of DesDiv 45 commanded by the redoubtable Captain Arleigh "30 Knot" Burke. Austin's staff recognized the silhouettes of the destroyers and, using the TBS[12] signalled:

> We've just had another close miss. Hope you are not shooting at us!

To which the reply was:

> Sorry but you'll have to excuse the next four salvoes — they're already on their way![13]

Why was *Spence* attacked? Visibility was clear and there should have been no difficulty in identifying *Spence* for what she was. Unfortunately *Spence's* IFF was not working, either through mechanical/electrical breakdown or enemy damage. Consequently she was identified as hostile and fired on. Fortunately visual identification corrected the error before any more damage or casualties were suffered and the destroyers turned their attention to the luckless *Hatsukaze*, sinking her. The lesson in that incident was quite clear: IFF could not be relied on totally and should be backed by visual identification.

The waters around Italy and the Dalmatian coast provided a fertile ground for errors in identification. Here the warships of four allied nations (Britain, the United States, France and co-belligerent Italy, after the 1943 Armistice) were operating together in fairly restricted waters. To add to this picture there were the activities of various "private" navies engaged in taking supplies to and from Tito's partisans in the former Yugoslavia. This was a situation where efficient and coherent staff work was required to keep all formations informed of the general picture, and it is a tribute to that staff work that there were so few incidents.

In the summer of 1943 the cruisers *Euryalus* and *Cleopatra* were on patrol close to the Sicilian coast when they encountered two MTBs heading south after a patrol. The cruisers challenged the MTBs and, when no reply was received, the cruisers fired starshell to illuminate the target and turned 90°away, the standard procedure to avoid torpedo attack. The MTBs fired torpedoes and there was a brief exchange of fire before the correct reply was given and order restored. There then occurred another of those exchange of signals which almost have the effect of turning such incidents into a black comedy:

> Cruiser: You are very lucky. I was about to blow you out of the water.
> MTB: You are even luckier, we've fired four torpedoes and missed.

MTBs were the "victims" in an incident in December, 1943, in the Adriatic. Following the German seizure of the island of Korcula, it was decided to evcuate the partisans and inhabitants on Lagosta to the island of Hvar on the grounds that Lagosta would be next to fall. Accordingly MTBs were used to evacuate the island on the night of 21/22 December, 1943. During the evacuation the MTBs reported that they:

> fought a spirited action with two of our own destroyers.[14]

The identity of the two British destroyers is unclear but HMS *Teazer* and HMS *Tyrian* were in the area at the time. The reason for the incident: lack of communication. The destroyers were unaware of the evacuation and probably identified the MTBs as *Schnellboote.*

The fast-moving and confused nature of engagements between coastal forces provided any number of occasions of friendly fire although it is difficult to find documented cases: in April, 1942, *MGBs 87, 88* and *89* operating from Lowestoft encountered boats from a sister flotilla based at Great Yarmouth. The boats from Lowestoft had strayed out of their area and compounded their mistake by giving the wrong reply on being challenged. The two boats from Yarmouth opened fire, raking *MGB. 87* and *MGB. 89* with 2 pdr fire, a formidable weapon against a boat with a frail wooden hull. Lieutenant S. B. Bennett DSC RN, commanding officer of *MGB. 89* and the coxswain were killed. Fortunately *MGB. 87* gave the correct reply before any further damage could be done but the incident illustrates the fast-moving nature of coastal forces' actions and the need for immediate and accurate recognition procedures.[15]

The *Kriegsmarine* were by no means immune from this sort of incident. On the night of 25/26 July, 1944, four *Schnellboote* of the 7th S-Boote Flotilla (*S. 151, S. 155, S. 156* and *S. 157*) were escorting a convoy consisting of the coaster *Vega* and two other vessels when they were attacked by *MTBs 651, 667* and *670* off Kanetza Island in the Adriatic. In the fierce mêlée that followed the *Schnellboote* succeeded in damaging *MTB. 651* before making their escape. To the amazement of the crews of the MTBs, two of the *Schnellboote,* one of which was *S. 151,* then engaged each other in a brief but intense gun duel. It is interesting to note that the British boats were showing their fighting lights, but the German vessels were not. As an amusing sequel to this incident, when one of the ships in the convoy exploded, she sent up a number of signal flares which must have made the correct signal since some shore batteries which had just opened up on the MTBs ceased fire!

One last instance from the Mediterranean/Adriatic theatre occurred on 6/7 October ,1944, when the Hunt class destroyer HMS *Whaddon* engaged *LCI(L). 290* off the Albanian coast, resulting in one rating killed and another wounded in the LCI. The primary cause of this incident was that *Whaddon* was unaware that the LCI, engaged in taking supplies/personnel into Albania, would be transitting her area. A secondary cause may well have been failure to recognize the silhouette of the LCI which bore a superficial resemblance to a *Kriegstransporter:* a flat bottomed craft used by the Germans for military supply duties.

The Royal Navy Motor Launch *ML. 251* was rammed and sunk, having been mistaken for a U-boat on 6 March, 1943. Fortunately there were no casualties, but the incident served as a reminder that, to be effective, a recognition signal must be seen by the ship for whom it is intended. The ML had sailed from the port of Bissau in West Africa early on the morning of 5 March for a routine anti-submarine patrol and had been expected to return to Freetown in the late afternoon, but for reasons which were never ascertained *ML. 251* did not return to Freetown when expected. At 1700 on the 5th the corvette HMS *Burdock* left Bissau, in company with her sister ship HMS *Thyme,* to escort a single merchant ship arriving from Freetown. The fact that *ML. 251* was still at sea was not passed to the two corvettes before they sailed.

At 2230 *Burdock* carried out an unsuccessful hunt for a submarine, but after obtaining a firm Asdic contact and plastering the area with depth charges, the search was abandoned when contact was lost. However, *Burdock's* crew believed that there had been a submarine in the area and were keyed up accordingly. Shortly after midnight on 6 March another contact was gained, this time on the surface. Believing this contact to be the same or another U-boat, *Burdock* turned in to ram and cut the other ship in two. Boats were lowered to collect any survivors and it was with some horror that the survivors were found to be the entire crew of *ML. 251.* She had been delayed in her anti-submarine patrol and was thus unaware of the presence of either the two corvettes or the merchant ship. Nevertheless, when *Burdock* was sighted the challenge was made by the commanding officer using a shaded blue lamp. When no reply was received and the other ship was seen turning on to a collision course, the ML's sole telegraphist was summoned to the bridge to make the challenge with a white light in plain language. But by then things had gone too far. The Board of Enquiry considered the following factors were responsible for the incident. Firstly that no concern had been expressed at Freetown when *ML. 251* did not arrive. Secondly the lack of information regarding the movements of other friendly ships. Thirdly that the commanding officer of the ML had made the challenge using a lamp of low intensity which could not be seen by those on *Burdock's* bridge and fourthly the state of lighting below decks in Burdock which was too bright, resulting in those coming on the bridge having eyesight unadapted to the dark. Nevertheless *Burdock's* commanding officer received a double commendation: firstly for his prompt action in rescuing all of *ML. 251's* crew and secondly for carrying out "an able and tenacious attack with the final turn to ram timed with nice precision!".[16]

The last two instances of this type both occurred in home waters. On the night of 27/28 May, 1944, the French frigate *La Combattante* was on E-boat patrol on latitude 50°22'N between 0°30'W and 0°45'W to cover Operation Fabius, one of the large invasion excercises which preceded the landings in Normandy. Also in the area was Unit F consisting of *MTB. 732* and *MTB. 739*. The sea was flat calm and both *La Combattante* and Unit F were being given their courses to steer from the shore. At 0100 on 28 May *La Combattante* obtained a radar contact and opened fire with main armament. The contact was in fact *MTB. 732* which received several hits and blew up with sixteen of her crew killed or missing and fifteen wounded. The Court of Enquiry concluded that the circumstances were the result of the hazards of war and that the incident, though tragic, reflected no discredit on the ships involved or the system. However, a number of points were made which are of interest. To begin with both parties were on the alert, looking for, and expecting, contact with the enemy. Having noted that insufficient use was made of IFF interrogators, despite the fact that both *La Combattante* and the MTBs were fitted with it. Secondly *La Combattante* and the MTBs were not on the same radio net: the MTBs were using the Coastal Forces Wave (2000 kc/s), while *La Combattante* was operating on 2450 kc/s. Thirdly *La Combattante's* signal office was overworked which led to a warning signal from CinC Portsmouth warning *La Combattante* that her targets were friendly being received too late.

Another misadventure of war concerned the attack on the cable-laying ship *Monarch* by the destroyer USS *Plunkett* off the Normandy beaches on 13 June, 1944. The destroyer was on routine patrol when at 0130 two ships were detected on radar approaching from the north. At roughly 0203 *Plunkett's* signals office "heard" one half of a radio conversation between their sister ship USS *Davis* in a the next "billet" about the identity of the ships.

However, the operators missed the "answer" and therefore doubt was created about the ships' identity.

At 0230, when the range had come down to 4,000 yards, a spread of starshell was fired but these failed to illuminate the target. Another spread was fired, but these too failed as they had been fired too low and hit the water before illuminating. At 0236 the left-hand of the two vessels was challenged, using the minor war vessel challenge but no reply was received. The challenge was repeated three times before *Plunkett* opened fire with her main armament. Shortly afterwards the second vessel was observed displaying the correct recognition lights and fire was checked. However, during this time the vessel fired on, the cable layer *Monarch* had been badly damaged with two killed, three seriously wounded and a number of other casualties.

*Monarch* had been engaged in the vital work of restoring cross-channel telephone cables. She was not fitted with recognition lights, nor did she carry the correct challenge and reply codes, as it was expected that all her work would be done offshore, under escort and in daylight. On this occasion her work had been held up by a defect in one of the cable barges and she was returning to her anchorage by night. The other ship was the Canadian corvette HMCS *Trentonian* and it was *Trentonian's* responsibility to protect her charge by carrying out the appropriate recognition procedures then in force. On this occasion *Trentonian* did not see any of *Plunkett's* four challenges, probably because they were made using a directional light. The first those on *Trentonian's* bridge knew of the incident was when *Plunkett's* shells fell around the *Monarch*.

The subsequent Board of Enquiry held that considerable enemy activity in *Plunkett's* area had caused the American ship to open fire somewhat sooner than was judged prudent but that no blame should be attached to any individual. The report concluded that the occurrence should be treated as a "misadventure of war" – a verdict to serve all such incidents.

In the heat of an action there was always the risk of a shell going "astray". On 12 October, 1942, the corvette *Petunia* chased a U-boat through the middle of a homeward-bound convoy firing at the submarine with her 4-inch gun. When in the middle of the convoy, *Petunia's* commanding officer withheld fire for fear of hitting one of the merchantmen and the the U-boat got away. The escort commander, Captain F. J. Walker, who later achieved fame in command of the Second Escort Group, considered that *Petunia's* actions had been half-hearted and that he should have continued the pursuit. In Walker's view the sinking of a U-boat far outweighed the risk of hitting a friendly merchant ship. Six months later those engaged in Atlantic convoys were less squeamish. On 17 April, 1943, *U-175* was sunk after a fierce gun battle with the US Coast Guard cutter *Spencer*. During the action the merchant ships of convoy HX. 223 joined in the firing and *Spencer* was struck by a 5-inch shell fired by one of the merchant ships. Fortunately no damage was done.

# CHAPTER FOUR

## *Aircraft vs Ships*

I must insist that everything possible is done in future to avoid
our own troops and units being confused with the enemy.

*Adolf Hitler after the loss of the German destroyer* Leberecht Maass.

Aircraft were the perpetrators of most friendly fire incidents at sea
during the Second World War whether the attacks were on warships, merchant ships or submarines. The reasons are not hard to
understand and go beyond the mere question of recognition. If
recognition is difficult for those on board ships, then the problems
are compounded for aircrew (particularly aircrew whose training
concentrated on operations in support of the army as was the case
with the *Luftwaffe*) by the greater speed of the aircraft, the weather
conditions (especially the light), errors in navigation and failures
in communication and intelligence. The boredom of long-range
patrols often led to targets being attacked simply out of excitement
before proper recognition procedures had been complied with.

In February, 1940, the German Navy planned an operation
against the British trawlers and drifters working the rich fishing
grounds off the Dogger Bank. The Germans thought that not only
would the raid force the Royal Navy to spread its escort forces even
further by having to guard the trawlers, but that the capture of a
trawler might yield useful intelligence. The operation was code-
named *Wikinger* and would be carried out by six destroyers led by
*Fregattenkapitän* Fritz von Berger flying his broad pendant in
*Friedrich Eckholdt,* accompanied by *Richard Beitzen, Theodore Riedel,*

*Max Schultze, Leberecht Maass* and *Erich Koellner.* The operation had been planned by the Navy's *Gruppe West* and co-ordinated with the *Luftwaffe's Fliegerkorps X,* who had promised fighter and bomber support during the short sortie. All concerned thought that the operation would be little more than a simple exercise. Events were to prove them very wrong.

The ships sailed from Schillig Roads at midday on 22 February and after passing to the south-west of Heligoland headed west-north-west for the six-mile-wide swept channel through the Westwall minefield. They received a report at 1830 from the *Führer des Luftwaffe West* that air reconnaissance revealed some sixty trawlers at sea south of Dogger Bank: the prospects looked good. The destroyers entered the minefield at 1900 in line ahead with *Eckholdt* leading, in order *Beitzen, Koellner, Riedel, Schultz* and *Maass.* The ships were 200 metres apart and steaming at 26 knots. Although it was cold, weather conditions were good with a light south-westerly wind and a low sea mist. The only disadvantage was that the moon lay dead astern, making the ships that much more detectable.

At 1913 the destroyers were overflown by an unidentified aircraft which flew up and down the line at a height of sixty metres as if trying to identify the ships. Berger was already concerned about the clearness with which the wakes of the ships stood out in the moonlight, so ordered speed to be reduced to 17 knots. At 1921 the aircraft appeared again: this time *Koellner* identified it as hostile, but *Maass* thought the aircraft was friendly. *Beitzen* and *Koellner* opened fire with 2cm AA guns, which was unfortunate, for it confirmed to the aircrew that the ships were hostile.

The aircraft was not sighted again until 1943 when *Maass* reported the plane coming in from astern and it was obvious that this time the aircraft was on an attacking run. Two bombs were dropped and one hit *Maass* between the bridge and forward funnel. The ship lost speed and slewed around to starboard, signalling for assistance. *Eckholdt* came back and stood off 500 metres from *Maass,* her crew breaking out towing gear, while Berger ordered the other destroyers which had also started to turn back to stay in line ahead, mindful of the width of the safe channel. Suddenly the aircraft came back and dropped another two bombs, one of which struck *Maass* between the funnels. When the smoke cleared all that

41

could be seen of the 1625-ton destroyer was her bow and stern sections pointing vertically upwards in the moonlight.

Berger now ordered all ships to lower boats to rescue *Maass's* survivors, swimming in the freezing oil-covered water. *Koellner* closed the wreck and lowered boats, as did *Eckholdt* and *Beitzen,* while *Riedel* and *Schultz* provided an anti-submarine screen. While all this was going on *Schultz* was suddenly engulfed in a terrific explosion. A state of panic erupted among the four remaining destroyers. *Riedel's* hydrophone operators announced contact with a submarine and four depth charges were dropped over the contact. Alas, *Riedel* was not moving fast enough to clear the radius of the depth-charge explosion and the shock of the three charges going off (one failed to detonate) caused considerable damage. *Leutnant zur See* Peter Cremer was *Riedel's* gunnery officer:

> When the lookout on the forward gun also reported "Bubble tracks sighted", indicating torpedoes, our Captain shouted "Make ready depth-charges" and seconds later, "Fire!" Four charges flew overboard in a high arc and the explosions shook us. Electric fuses jumped out, and as an unexpected side-effect, the electric steering gear was momentarily jammed. *Theodore Riedel* began to rotate like a circus horse.[1]

Submarines and torpedoes were now being sighted everywhere and neither Berger nor anyone else had a clear idea of what was going on. *Koellner* attempted to ram the "submarine" only to find that it was the upturned bow of the *Maass,* still afloat. In the confusion *Koellner* had ordered her motor boat to be cast off, but had increased speed before this had been done and the boat was dragged under her wake, drowning its hapless crew. Through the confusion Berger grasped that two of his destroyers were sunk and ordered the force to return to Wilhelmshaven. This was a major disaster for the *Kriegsmarine.* Only sixty of of *Maass'* complement of 330 were saved and there were no survivors at all from *Schultz.* Most had drowned in the bitterly cold water. Two brand-new destroyers, vitally important units in view of forthcoming operations in Norway, had been sunk.

42

Sorting out what had happened was appallingly difficult, since everyone's views on what had happened differed so radically. Initially, the RAF was held responsible: after all *Koellner* had identified the aircraft as hostile. However, this answer lacked all credibility given the RAF's singular lack of success against surface ships: that they could sink two in a night was stretching belief. On the other hand the aircraft had definitely been identified as German by *Maass,* and it was only when reports came in from the headquarters of *Fliegerkorps X* that one of their aircraft had attacked ships steering 300°, 20 miles north of the Terschelling lightship, that the awful truth began to dawn on *Gruppe West.*

At first the idea that a "friendly" aircraft was responsible was discarded by both *Kriegsmarine* and *Luftwaffe.* At the Führer's naval conference the next morning at which were present Hitler, *Generalfeldmarschall* Wilhelm Keitel, head of the *Oberkommando der Wehrmacht* (the German High Command), *Grossadmiral* Erich Raeder, commander in chief of the *Kriegsmarine* and *Fregattenkapitän* Otto von Puttkamer, Hitler's naval ADC, Raeder announced somewhat lamely that:

> During an operation by a destroyer flotilla off the Dogger Bank on the evening of 22 February for the purpose of bringing in British steam trawlers, two destroyers were lost. The cause has not been discovered but German aircraft may be responsible.[2]

It was Hitler who ordered an enquiry which met that day on board the cruiser *Admiral Hipper* under the chairmanship of *Generalmajor* Coeler of the *Luftwaffe* and included *Kapitän zur See* Heye of the *Kriegsmarine* and *Oberstleutnant* Lobel, commanding officer of *KG. 30.* Aircrew, survivors and officers and men of the surviving destroyers were all interviewed at length. The Enquiry revealed an appalling lack of co-operation between the staffs of *Fliegerkorps X* and *Gruppe West.* The story of events as discovered by the Enquiry was as follows. On the morning of 22 February *Fliergerkorps X* informed Gruppe West that they intended, in view of the fine weather, to employ 1 Staffel of KG. 26 in anti-shipping operations south of the Humber and in the Channel. The sorties would be

43

timed so that the aircraft would be in their operational areas by 1930. The operational orders were given to *Gruppe West* by telephone at 1218[3] on the 22nd and confirmed by teleprinter at 1430. In the meantime the *Kriegsmarine* were mounting operation *Wikinger* but took no steps to alert the staff of *Fliegerkorps X* until 1735 when they requested that air operations should be prohibited from an area north of the Terschelling lightship, south of 55°N and east of the British declared minefield, since German destroyers would be operating in this area. However, this message arrived too late to be passed to the aircrew of KG. 26.

That night and early the next morning, signals were received from Berger and from KG. 26 which indicated the confused state of events at sea. At 2030 Berger signalled to *Gruppe West* that *Maass* had been sunk and followed this signal with another at 2102 to the effect that *Schultz* was also missing and that he believed a submarine to be responsible. At 2300 the staff of *Fliergerkorps X* reported that a 3,000-ton steamer had been attacked and sunk north of Terschelling. It was not until the morning of 23 February when the *Kriegsmarine* finally admitted that the sinking, "might have something to do with our own aircraft".[4] The *Kriegsmarine* took a remarkably relaxed view of the affair, noting no more than that the incident was:

> a consequence of the joint organization in the North Sea
> where two Wehrmacht services share responsibility for
> the conduct of the war.[5]

The Enquiry concluded that, as a result of this mess, the attacks on the Maass could be attributed to aircraft HIM, an He-111 torpedo bomber, of 4/KG. 26 which had confused the destroyer with a merchant ship. The Enquiry also noted that:

> This night attack was the first which this crew had ever
> undertaken. Experience of this kind of operation,
> including recognizing and determining a target, was
> also lacking. It was only their second ever night flight
> over sea and as such they suffered from lack of experi-
> ence in managing navigational data.

The crew of the aircraft were not informed of the possibility of encountering German vessels.[6]

In other words the two destroyers were sunk because of a lethal combination of poor staffwork and inexperience among the aircrew. It might be worth noting at this stage that it was a superb performance for an untrained crew to attack and sink a ship while flying at night on their first sortie! The Enquiry concluded that:

In every case, a continuous and extensive briefing of the higher staffs appears necessary. There are no complaints about the conduct of the aircraft or the destroyers.[7]

The findings were presented on 4 March. They were accepted by the *Seekriegsleitung,* but *Gruppe West* was not convinced. Admiral Alfred Saalwachter, Commander in Chief of *Gruppe West,* replied to Raeder that it was impossible to brief every ship under his command about air operations:

The destroyers knew that the appearance of friendly aircraft was constantly to be reckoned with. A continuous briefing could never make matters clearer since various air force units appeared in the area without the knowledge of the *Gruppe.*[8]

Moreover, as Saalwachter pointed out, the aircraft had disobeyed standing orders which forbade indiscriminate air attacks on blacked-out vessels unless they were clearly identified as hostile. This was a very inadequate excuse and did nothing to explain the low quality of *Gruppe West's* staff work. The aircrew were untrained in the art of night attacks over water and would have had great difficulty in identifying the ships. Moreover the light flak offered by *Beitzen* and *Koellner* would have given the unfortunate aircrew positive indication that the ships were hostile.

While the official enquiry was taking evidence, Hitler had already issued a directive on the subject since he was clearly unhappy with the preliminary findings. It is not often possible to agree with Hitler but on this occasion his directive cuts to the heart of things:

In the war up to now, the Wehrmacht has repeatedly suffered noticeable losses from friendly fire (*Eigene
Waffenwirkung*). It is quite clear to me that frictions and
misunderstandings are never entirely avoidable in war.
I must insist that everything possible is done in future
to avoid our own troops and units being confused with
the enemy.

To this end:

1.  A flawless reciprocal briefing of command
    authorities of all grades on the movements on
    land, sea and air taking place in the same oper-
    ational area.
2.  Tightened regulations on the giving of recog-
    nition signals in all situations where friend and
    enemy might be confused.
3.  I cannot tolerate that, instead of reciprocal help,
    there are still heavy losses.[9]

In the light of postwar research the findings of the Board can be
disputed. Although there is no doubt that the He-111 was responsible for sinking *Maass,* doubts have arisen over whether or not
*Schultz* too was sunk by the *Luftwaffe.* The "safe" channel had in
fact been mined by two British destroyers on the night of 9/10
February. Given that the channel had not been "swept" since then,
those mines would have been there and active. *Schultz,* therefore,
may have strayed into this British minefield. Admiral Saalwachter
raised this argument on 30 November, 1940, claiming both ships
had been mined on account of the fact that he doubted whether
three 50kg bombs could have sunk the *Maass.* It was all very spec-
ulative and represented a rather shallow attempt to clear *Gruppe
West's* role in the affair. The fact remains that, even if both ships
did run onto British mines, they did so in the confusion attending
a bombing run by one of their own aircraft.

The hunt for the German battleship Bismarck in May, 1941,
provided one of the best known incidents of mistaken identity by
aircraft which nearly ended in disaster. *Bismarck* having evaded her
shadowers, contact was regained by an RAF Coastal Command
Catalina flying boat at 1030 on 26 May. Heading north from

46

Gibraltar was Force H consisting of the battlecruiser HMS *Renown*, aircraft carrier HMS *Ark Royal* and cruiser HMS *Sheffield*, the whole under command of Vice Admiral Sir James Somerville flying his flag in *Renown*. Subsequently *Bismarck* was reported by two reconnaissance Swordfish from *Ark Royal* and preparations began for a torpedo attack.

At 1300 Somerville ordered *Sheffield* (Captain C. Larcom RN) to increase speed to close the *Bismarck*, then estimated to be 40 miles from Renown, to make contact and report her course and speed:

> *Sheffield* lifted her bows as she smashed into the swell, and on both flanks and astern the sea creamed. In the boiler rooms below, the fans were roaring, burners and turbines screamed, artificers among the labyrinth of ladders, catwalks and asbestos-covered pipes watched their brass-rimmed gauges. Within minutes the paint on both funnels began to blister and peel. By 1500 the cruiser was steaming at 31.5 knots and increasing, the wind WSW, force 6. At 1630 it was piped: "The ship is now steaming at 38 knots," which was six knots more than her engines had been designed for.[10]

Having detached *Sheffield*, Somerville had to let *Ark Royal* know of his action in order that the carrier's aircrew would know of the presence of a friendly ship between them and *Bismarck*. At the time *Ark Royal* was beyond visual signalling range so *Renown* contacted the shore station at Portishead on ship/shore HF to inform the Admiralty, in cipher, of *Sheffield's* departure. The signal was to be repeated to C in C Home Fleet and to *Ark Royal*. The procedure was cumbersome but it was the surest way of ensuring that *Ark Royal* was aware of the position of friendly ships.

However, when the signal was received in *Ark Royal* it was not dealt with immediately. The aircraft carrier's W/T office were dealing with a backlog of traffic and Somerville's signal which was seen as repeated to *Ark Royal* "for information" was left to be deciphered later. Thus when at 1450 the fourteen aircraft[11] of 820 Squadron took off for a strike on the *Bismarck*, their crews knew nothing of

47

*Sheffield's* presence. The first ship they sighted, they were briefed, would be *Bismarck.*

Commander J. Stewart-Moore RN was 820 Squadron's commanding officer:

> The aircraft next to mine in the leading sub-flight carried one of the first airborne radar sets – ASV – manned by a young sub-lieutenant, Lithgow, and an even younger midshipman, Cooper. The latter's duties included navigation, radar operator, wireless operator and general look-out. After a while I saw Cooper waving to me – he semaphored that he had a radar contact about 20 miles to starboard. We were told that there were no British ships in the area so it had to be German.
>
> We saw what appeared to be a cruiser. We approached above clouds getting occasional glimpses, and decided to attack. After dropping torpedoes my pilot, Hunter, called down the voicepipe "It's the *Sheffield.*" Hunter waggled our wings to attract the attention of other aircraft, but couldn't prevent some of them attacking while we watched from above, horrified and praying for a miracle.[12]

*Ark Royal's* aircrew were thoroughly familiar with the *Sheffield;* the two ships had steamed thousands of miles together in company. Moreover *Bismarck* was five times the cruiser's tonnage, was nearly 300 feet longer and had one funnel as opposed to *Sheffield's* two. It might seem impossible for the aircrew to fail to identify *Sheffield* but they only saw what they expected to see.

*Sheffield* was the only ship in Force H equipped with radar but had it switched off at this time for fear of the Germans picking up the transmissions. Sub-Lieutenant Al Hurley RCNVR was *Sheffield's* radar officer:

> I will always remember the words coming down the voicepipe that the *Ark's* bombers were sighted, and then the excited retort, "My God, they're attacking us!"[13]

Captain Larcom called for emergency full speed and ordered the AA armament to refrain from firing. Hurley had left the radar office and gone up on the bridge to be better able to observe proceedings:

> Larcom was a cool customer. As each group of three aircraft lined up to make a run at us he would bring *Sheffield* beam on to their approach hoping they would recognize our profile. When they failed to do so and dropped their torpedoes, he had to bring the ship round smartly to meet the fish head on. We had just avoided one such attack on the port bow when I saw, from my vantage point, another three forming up to starboard. I could not resist shouting "There are three more attacking on the starboard bow, sir!" – which was a bit presumptuous for a sub-lieutenant RCNVR, Special Branch, from a position which I should never have been in in the first place.[14]

Only three pilots realized their mistake and abandoned their attack. The remainder all released their torpedoes. Fortunately five of the torpedoes, fitted with duplex magnetic pistols, exploded prematurely, and the remainder were avoided by Larcom's consummate ship-handling, thus preventing the first "radar-assisted own goal".

Meanwhile *Ark Royal's* signals office were sorting themselves out. During the return flight to *Ark Royal* Stewart-Moore was handed a signal by his wireless operator, Petty Officer R. H. McColl:

> handed me a message, "Operational Immediate – Look out for *Sheffield* which is in your vicinity." I thought of plenty of rude replies but none seemed helpful, except perhaps 1 Kings X v. 7: "Behold, the half was not told me!" I did not send it.[15]

The proposed signal could stand as an epitaph for so many such incidents.

Aircrew trained for land operations in support of armies, as was the case for most of the *Luftwaffe*, had particular problems when suddenly deployed on maritime operations. In the spring of 1941 *Fliergerkorps IV* was deployed to the Mediterranean to support Axis naval units engaged in the invasion of Crete. There they found themselves employed in an unfamiliar role and working with their allies, the Italians, with all the added problems of language and different procedures.

22 May, 1941, was a day of ill omen for Axis co-operation in the Mediterranean. The Italian destroyer *Sagittario* was escorting a convoy of caiques when she was engaged by the British Force C (cruisers *Naiad, Perth Calcutta* and *Carlisle;* destroyers *Kandahar, Kingston* and *Nubian),* south of the island of Milos. *Sagittario* under the command of *Capitan di Fregata* Cigala-Fulgosi, fought a brilliant delaying action against superior odds aided by constant bombing attacks by Ju-88s of 1/LG. 1 and III/KG. 30 and Do-17s of KG. 2. *Sagittario* drew the the British destroyers away from the convoy and then broke away using her superior speed. On rejoining the convoy Sagittario was dive-bombed by Ju-88s: five bombs were dropped but none hit. It was later admitted that the German aircrew had attacked because, understandably, they felt that a ship closing the convoy at high speed was bound to be hostile.

When news of the action was received at Piraeus a convoy of four Italian destroyers (*Sella, Lince, Libra* and *Monzambano),* which had just sailed for Suda Bay in Crete carrying German mountain troops, was ordered to return owing to the uncertain situation. While on their way back the ships were attacked by a lone Ju-87 which bombed the *Sella,* the bombing missing the ship but peppering her side with splinters. The aircraft then machine-gunned the Sella, killing six and wounding twenty-three: most of the casualties were among the embarked (German) troops. *Sella* opened fire and the aircraft was shot down.

The incident was intensely annoying to the Italians since not only did it come almost immediately after the bombing of *Sagittario* but also because the Germans had failed to provide air cover for the convoy whose sailing orders had been issued by the (German) port captain at Piraeus. For their part the *Luftwaffe* said the bombing was due to the heat of the battle where aircraft were repeatedly engaged in a series of attacks on shipping – a lame excuse at the best of times.

Co-operation between the Italians and the Germans barely improved throughout the rest of the war. On 15 June, 1942, an Italian squadron of two cruisers and five destroyers was attacked by a mixed force of German and Italian dive bombers while waiting in ambush for a convoy headed for Malta, operation *Harpoon*. The Italian force had in fact been in action with the convoy earlier in the morning but had broken off the action and steamed ahead to wait for the convoy at a position where it would have to exit from a minefield: they waited in vain, for the convoy took a more southerly course. However, they were attacked twice from the air, firstly by a force of Blenheim torpedo bombers from Malta and then by their own side. Details of any damage or casualties sustained are not known.

Later that afternoon the British destroyer *Bedouin*, which had been badly damaged in the morning's engagement with the cruisers, sank. An Italian hospital ship began rescue work at 2100 only to be bombed by an Italian aircraft for her pains. Both these incidents were obviously due to failure of recognition but also to the lack of intelligence at shore headquarters of the swiftly developing nature of the action, and that friendly units would not always be where the staff thought they should be.

Difficulties between allies were not a monopoly of the Axis side. On 9 May, 1943, the Hunt class destroyer HMS *Bicester*, in company with HMS *Zetland*, was patrolling off the Tunisian coast to prevent the escape of the remnants of the Axis army from North Africa. When off Zembra Island at 0830 *Bicester* was bombed and machine-gunned by three USAAC Spitfires. Although the ship was not hit she was damaged aft by a near miss which caused flooding to the waterline between 134 and 108 bulkheads. *Bicester*'s commanding officer was a character well known for his ability to convey maximum effect in his signals. Using the radio, he was able to convince the American pilots that his ship was "allied but no longer friendly" and so prevented further attacks. She was escorted to Sousse for temporary repairs (where a second unexploded bomb was found in an oil fuel tank) but permanent repairs had to be carried out in the UK.

In an attempt to prevent a repeat of the incident, the RAF asked that ships withdraw from the coastline during daylight. This was subsequently modified to ships being prohibited from coming within five miles of the coastline (although this distance would be almost impossible to judge from a fast single-seat aircraft). Additionally ships were to paint the upper surfaces of their bridge superstructures a distinguishing colour.

Errors in navigation were common, particularly over the sea, and hard to avoid given the rudimentary equipment available to navigators. Problems arose when aircraft strayed into the operational area of other friendly forces, especially areas which had been declared a Total Bombing Restriction area. Land-based aircrew were also likely to be unfamiliar with the general modus operandi of both own and enemy forces. On 4 May, 1944, *MTBs 708* and *720* were off St Catherine's Point on the southern tip of the Isle of Wight, heading for Portland after completing a patrol. At 0717 a large group of Beaufighters passed down their port side about one and a half miles away. Since the MTBs were in a bombing restriction zone, no recognition signal was made. In retrospect a recognition signal might have saved the two craft for a number of aircraft peeled away from the formation and delivered diving attacks on the MTBs with cannon fire before *MTB. 708* managed to fire the correct recognition signal. But the damage was done: *MTB. 708* was riddled with cannon fire and had to be scuttled. *MTB. 720* was also damaged but succeeded in reaching Portland. Seventeen officers and men were wounded, ten of them seriously.

The Commander in Chief Portsmouth commented that the principal cause of the incident was an error in navigation by the Beaufighters which brought them closer to the bombing restriction area used by the MTBs. He added that a supplementary reason was that the Beaufighters were new to maritime operations and therefore did not appreciate that it was highly unlikely that German ships would be almost within sight of the British coast in daylight.

Aircraft operating in support of the Army in the Far East faced additional problems of navigation over the largely featureless jungle terrain. This was the reason behind the deaths of nine officers and men and another eighteen wounded in October, 1944. During the typhoon season all naval forces were withdrawn from the Arakan front except for three motor launches (MLs) and six landing craft which were employed in several small operations for the Army. On 7 October, 1944, *ML. 1118* and *ML. 1119* were at anchor at Muangdaw on the Naaf River when they were attacked by two Spitfires and subjected to heavy cannon and machine-gun fire. *ML. 1119* was sunk and *ML. 1118* badly damaged. Not only had the Spitfires mistaken them for enemy ships but the pilots thought they were over the Mayu instead of the Naaf River.

# CHAPTER FIVE

## Aircraft vs Ships (ii)
## & Ships vs Aircraft

It is felt that the fury and ferocity of concerted attacks by a
number of Typhoon aircraft, armed with rockets and cannons,
is an ordeal that has to be be endured to be truly appreciated.

*Commander Trevor Crick DSC RN, Commanding Officer of*
*HMS Jason*

The worst such incident involving attacks on friendly ships by air-
craft occurred off the French coast following the invasion of
Normandy in June, 1944, when ships of the 1st Minesweeping
Flotilla (1st MSF) were deliberately attacked by rocket-firing RAF
Typhoon fighter bombers. HMS *Hussar* and *Britomart* were sunk,
HMS *Salamander* so badly damaged that she was beyond repair and
two other ships damaged. Seventy-eight officers and ratings were
killed and 149 wounded, many seriously.

The ships of the flotilla had been deployed off the Normandy
beaches since the beginning of the invasion. On 5 and 6 June the
ships had swept channels through to Sword Beach for Assault
Convoy S1 and thereafter had been employed in routine clearance
of the swept channel between Portsmouth and Arromanches.
However, on 22 August the Flotilla was ordered to clear a field of
German magnetic mines laid five miles off the French coast
between Fécamp and Cap d'Antifer. The clearance of this minefield would enable the battleship HMS *Warspite* and the monitors
*Erebus* and *Roberts* to move close to the shore and bombard German

positions around Le Havre in preparation for the assault on the city by the Canadians. After four days of work clearing this field, the Flotilla, now reduced to *Jason* (SO), *Britomart, Hussar* and *Salamander*,[1] enjoyed a rest day at Arromanches.

On the evening of the 25th Commander Trevor Crick DSC RN, Commanding Officer of HMS *Jason* and senior officer of the Flotilla (the Commanding Officer of the Flotilla was away) received orders that the Flotilla was to return to their previous work of clearing the Portsmouth/Arromanches channel on the morning of the 27th. Lieutenant H. G. S. Brownbill RNR was *Jason*'s navigating officer:

> We knew full well that the clearance and search of the area off Le Havre had not been completed and we also knew that clearance was urgently needed to permit a heavy force to use the area to bombard the Le Havre coastal region. Commander Crick and I discussed the position and on his orders I went on board the mine-sweeping headquarters ship *Ambitious* to query the orders with the staff of Captain Minesweepers. I was not received with any particular enthusiasm as all the staff officers were at supper. However, I made my point and was promised that the orders would be amended to allow the 1st MSF to complete its unfinished search and clearance. Happy that all was in hand I returned to *Jason*.[2]

What should have happened next was for the Flotilla staff to circulate the amended orders to other service commands. It was essential that all shipping movements off the French coast be disclosed, not just to other naval commands but also to the relevant Army and Air Force commands, in order to prevent misunderstandings.

The signal amending the Flotilla's orders was received in *Jason* early on the morning of Sunday 27 August, shortly before the ships weighed anchor for the day's operations. It was a fine day with almost perfect conditions for minesweeping. *Britomart, Jason* and *Salamander* were abreast of each other with Salamander nearest the shore. Astern of *Britomart* came *Hussar* whose sweep gear was defective. Inshore of *Salamander* was the trawler *Colsay* which was laying DAN buoys to mark the swept channels, while the trawler *Lord Ashfield,* another DAN layer, steamed astern.

Shortly before noon an RAF aircraft made a low pass over the ships, the pilot acknowledging the waves from members of the ships' companies idling on deck. In HMS *Britomart*, Les Williams recalled that:

> It was a perfect day. Most of *Britomart's* crew were sunbathing on the upper deck. Even the duty watch were stripped off at their guns.[3]

The Flotilla had just begun the third leg of their sweep at about 1330 when a group of aircraft came diving down out of the sun and attacked *Britomart.* Les Williams remembered that:

> When the lookout shouted, "Aircraft on the port side," everybody got up, but we couldn't see anything because the sun was shining straight into our eyes. Then the lookout called, "They're friendly aircraft". I saw the planes diving towards us. The black and white stripes which Allied aircraft had in those days were quite plain, so we thought they were just making a practice attack. Then suddenly I saw flashes coming from their wings. I yelled "Duck!" and flung myself down the nearest hatch, about six feet away.[4]

The aircraft were clearly recognized as Typhoons and Crick reported at once that his ships were being attacked by friendly aircraft and repeated the signal two minutes later at 1334. The attack took *Britomart* by surprise. All the officers not on watch were gathered in the wardroom diciphering signals when:

> two great explosions shocked the entire ship by their power and violence, smashing, shattering, shuddering. My immediate thought was that we had been mined for'ard, but three seconds later, before we had time to collect ourselves, two more explosions sounded under the quarterdeck on the port side. The ship lurched over

to starboard and rolled back to settle with a ten degree list to port ... We bundled out on deck only to fall flat on our faces when greeted by a second burst of cannon fire from an aircraft streaking past to starboard – we were horrified to see that it was an RAF Typhoon.[5]

John Price was a telegraphist in HMS *Britomart*:

My first thought was "What the hell are the silly bastards playing at?", and this was overtaken by the thought that they were using us as an exercise target. Then from under the aircraft I could see a red burst, and then there was a loud, dull thump and out of the corner of my eye I saw it hit our bridge. My first thought was self-preservation and I moved to crawl under the gun platform. Unfortunately it was only about three inches off the deck and I was a bit too large, so I tumbled down the hatchway in the wardroom flat ... Things went very quiet at this stage, and I recall seeing one seaman with the lower half of his face shot away. I have a hazy recollection that his wife had given birth to a child some days previously. Another recollection is of the ship crippled and canting round to one side going round in circles like a dog chasing its tail.[6]

The Typhoon attack literally ripped *Britomart* apart. The bridge and funnel were destroyed and the upper deck had been turned into a mass of twisted metal so that it was impossible for anyone at the after end of the ship to go forward and vice versa. The Engineer Officer, Warrant Officer J. R. D. Gregson, gallantly severed the Double L sweep that the ship was towing, which was still pumping out 5000 amps into the water, by cutting it with an axe. Lieutenant Commander H. Johnson, an officer embarked in *Britomart* to gain minesweeping experience while awaiting an appointment to his own command, but who found himself as senior surviving officer, decided that he had no choice but to order the crew to abandon ship. It was clear that *Britomart* was beyond salvage and, moreover, she was drifting helplessly in the middle of a minefield.

57

Astern of *Britomart* was HMS *Hussar* commanded by Lieutenant Commander John Nash MBE RNR:

> The first thing we saw was *Britomart* being attacked and badly hit, then it was our turn. On seeing they were RAF planes we tried to fire the recognition signal but the Very pistol jammed.[7]

*Hussar's* bridge was raked with rocket and cannon fire. Her navigating officer was killed instantly and Lieutenant Commander Nash was severely wounded in both legs and the right arm where his elbow was shot away. All communication with the engine room was lost, but a rating courageously used the emergency stop lever situated in the cross-passage for'ard of the wardroom to alert the engine room staff to stop the engines. .

Leading Stoker Hal Booth was off watch and had been sunbathing on the upper deck at the time of the attack:

> I had dozed off but woke up suddenly at a strange noise and saw the minesweeper ahead of us (*Britomart*) surrounded by a mass of little waterspouts with a plane diving on her. We jumped up and ran – there were men running on all sides. As we dashed down the ladder to the mess deck the action bells sounded and I ran to my action station in the engine room but before I could get there the whole engine room area was aflame after being hit by rockets and in the passage outside a lot of washing hung up to dry was burning fiercely. Grabbing an extinguisher I put out the flames, then tried to get into the engine room. Inside all was utter chaos with men lying dead and others terribly injured, one man with both legs smashed.[8]

Coder Stan Timothy had also been among those taking it easy on the upper deck:

> Just afterwards *Hussar* gave a tremendous shudder and started to heel over to port. The degaussing and

electrical systems were damaged and I thought we had been hit by a magnetic mine. We – the wireless staff – managed to get up to the upper deck which was now at an angle of 45 degrees, and as some of the upper super-structure was breaking away, I made for the starboard rail. Climbing up the sloping deck I noticed that a hatch cover was moving and was able to help those inside by loosening a spring wire which was fouling it. A head appeared and a voice said, "About time too!" I slid down the starboard side and swam away with others of the crew.[9]

Lieutenant Commander Nash was one of the last to leave the ship:

Because of my wounds I was not feeling too good. When the planes attacked I was not wearing a lifebelt, so now I took a self-inflatable one from a dead officer and when the bridge rail was level with the sea, stepped into it, but at that very moment *Hussar* decided to turn turtle and part of the rigging caught me across the back and took me down with it. Luckily, somehow or other I got free and kicked my way to the surface.[10]

*Hussar* sank by the stern with her bows above water. It had taken less than twelve minutes for the little minesweeper to sink.

The last ship to be hit was HMS *Salamander* (Lieutenant Commander H. G. King RNR). As the Typhoons attacked *Brito-mart* and *Hussar,* King ordered the red and green recognition flares to be fired, while a large Union Jack was spread out on deck. It was to no avail. A Typhoon, covered by two others, approached from astern and let fly a salvo of rockets which hit the depth charges stowed on the ship's stern. The resulting explosion blew the stern away and left the sweep deck a mass of charred and tangled metal.

By 1342 the attack was over. It had lasted no more than twelve minutes. From *Jason's* bridge Commander Crick surveyed the remains of his Flotilla. *Britomart* was burning badly and listing heavily to port. *Hussar* had sunk leaving only the tip of her bows above the water. *Salamander* was drifting helplessly with a severe fire engulfing her stern. Crick's own ship had been raked by cannon fire as had the trawlers *Colsay* and *Lord Ashley*. Crick could do no more than wireless an immediate request for tugs and begin to pick up the survivors.

The *Colsay* was rescuing men from the *Britomart,* so Crick took *Jason* over to where *Hussar's* survivors were swimming in the water. As rescue work commenced both ships came under fire from German shore batteries who had been passive witnesses of the sequence of events. Crick had no choice but to retire out of gun range and order *Colsay* to do the same and then send back small boats to pick up those still in the water, but the shelling was accurate and took a heavy toll.

> All my men in the water had drifted away a little closer
> to the shore when the German shells started exploding
> all around. Shrapnel from the shells, which burst on
> impact with the water, killed many men, by hitting
> them in the head. This was the most dreadful part, a har-
> rowing scene.[11]

Lieutenant Commander Johnson from *Britomart* was picked up by a whaler:

> We were transferred to an RAF launch on which there
> were some pretty terrifying cases, but all displaying
> amazing courage. There was a Petty Officer from
> *Hussar* with not only his right arm and shoulder miss-
> ing but a good part of his rib cage too. He was half
> lying, half sitting, chain smoking, with this dreadful
> mess exposed to a glaring sun. I dropped a wet hanker-
> chief over it but he said, "It doesn't matter, I can't feel
> it anyway".[12]

Meanwhile *Salamander* was drifting helplessly toward the French coast and the shore batteries. Very quickly Commander Crick laid a two-mile smokescreen between *Salamander* and the shore before taking her in tow. By now other units were arriving on the scene. The Hunt class destroyer HMS *Pytchley* carried a medical officer and she began to accept the wounded from the other rescue ships. Ships of the 6th Minesweeping Flotilla, which were sweeping nearby, also rendered assistance. On board HMS *Gozo* was Able Seaman Trevor Davies:

> As we got up to them, we edged in very slowly, there were lots of men in the water, some dead, others trying to escape from the oil which surrounded them. We threw lines to men in the water and to others in a whaler and helped them on board. All were covered in oil, coughing and choking. Everyone on *Gozo* was doing our best although we ourselves were all devastated and heartbroken by what had happened.[13]

At 1500 the rescue work was complete. *Britomart* had turned right over and so *Pytchley* was ordered to sink her with gunfire along with *Hussar.* The rescue ships then returned to Arromanches, *Jason* stopping en route to bury her dead. At Arromanches the wounded were transferred to hospital ships and the other survivors to Army camps ashore before being sent back to Portsmouth. There they were thoroughly debriefed and sent on the usual fourteen days survivors' leave with a strict injunction not to say anything of their ordeal: it was an order most were only too happy to obey. Other attempts at damage limitation were more inventive. On board HMS *Gozo,* the commanding officer cleared lower deck and thanked the ship's company for their rescue work:

> I remember that he said, "Yes, the Typhoons and Spitfires were British, but these had been captured and flown by the Germans. Somehow that statement made us feel better and we all agreed that it was the bastard Germans and just increased our hate for them.[14]

After arriving in Portsmouth some days after the attack John Price was told:

> that a group of German ships had left Le Havre the previous night, ie Saturday night, and that they had been

attacked. Moving up the coast as we were and not seeing us turn at the river mouth it was assumed that we
had just left Le Havre, therefore we must be German and
the attack was ordered.[15]

In his diary for 28 August, Admiral Sir Bertram Ramsay, the
Allied Naval CinC, wrote:

The worst news was the sinking of 2 M/S & damaging
of another by our own aircraft due, I fear, to a mistake
or otherwise on FOBAA's part.[16]

Ramsay lost no time in ordering an enquiry into what had happened. The Enquiry found that the primary cause of the disaster
was the failure of the staff on board HMS *Ambitious,* the
minesweepers' headquarters ship, to inform the Flag Officer
British Assault Area (FOBAA), Rear Admiral J. W. Rivett-Carnac,
of the change made on the evening of 26 August to the following
day's minesweeping programme. As a result FOBAA's staff were
unware that the 1st MSF would be in the area. The actual mistake
consisted of a staff officer forgetting to write "(R)FOBAA"
(Repeated to FOBAA) on the signal amending 1st MSFs operational orders.

On the morning of 27 August the ships of the 1st MSF were
detected by a shore radar station and were identified as hostile since
the orders for that day indicated no "friendly" ships operating in
that area. An RAF reconnaissance was ordered to confirm the identity of the ships and reported a force of minesweepers and trawlers
which "appeared to be friendly".[17] The RAF consulted FOBAA's
staff who confirmed that no friendly ships were in the area.
However, in view of doubt raised by the pilot's identification of the
ships as *possibly* friendly, FOBAA's staff attempted to contact HMS
*Ambitious* to confirm that none of the minesweepers were in the
area. Owing to a breakdown in telephone communications, this
enquiry was never received and FOBAA's staff did not press the
matter or try alternative means of communication.

Accordingly a flight of eight Typhoons of 263 and 266

(Rhodesia) Squadrons RAF took off from landing strip B3 in France under the command of Wing Commander J. Baldwin DSO DFC AFC. Baldwin was an extremely experienced Typhoon pilot, who had been responsible for the attack on the staff car carrying Field Marshal Erwin Rommel in which Rommel was badly wounded, and who had chased two Fw. 190s around the Eifel Tower. Baldwin lacked nothing when it came to aggressiveness but was unhappy at his orders to attack shipping which had been provisionally identified as "friendly". Twice in the air he questioned his orders but when confronted with a definite order to proceed he had no choice.

The Enquiry found that, "Staff work fell short of the highest standards in several respects"[18] and made certain recommendations for disciplinary action. Three officers were court-martialled at Rouen for their role in the affair. FOBAA's Staff Officer Operations and Captain Minesweepers Seine Bay were both acquitted, the latter having been away on the day in question. The deputy to Captain Minesweepers Seine Bay was also court-martialled, found guilty of negligence and severely reprimanded.

With studied understatement, Commander Crick noted in his report that:

> It is felt that the fury and ferocity of concerted attacks by a number of Typhoon aircraft armed with rockets and cannons is an ordeal that has to be be endured to be truly appreciated.[19]

Crick received an OBE for his "coolness, courage and devotion to duty" but as he said in a newspaper interview in 1962, "It certainly was a queer way to get a gong."[20] The loss of these two little minesweepers was deeply felt in the wider community of the Royal and Merchant Navies. For nearly three years these little ships had been a constant presence in the Arctic where British ships struggled through atrocious weather and fierce enemy opposition to bring supplies to a seemingly ungrateful Soviet ally. *Britomart* and her sisters had been based in Murmansk and were general maids of all work, performing many other roles in addition to the minesweeping for which they had been designed. Their presence was a welcome sight to mariners arriving in the dismal surroundings of the Kola Inlet. That they had met their end in such an ignoble fashion was the cause of much sadness as news of their fate spread throughout the fleet.

When describing the events fifty years later, John Price of HMS *Britomart*, wrote:

> The initial feeling when the attack starts is one of anger. I am sure that there were a good many ratings that day who were raging in their hearts against "those stupid bastards" who couldn't distinguish a White Ensign from a German flag. Going out on deck to wave your fist at them would, I fear, have been tempting fate. This rage does stay with you for a long time.
>
> On reflection, much later, you realize that with no wind and an ensign hanging down like a dirty duster, they couldn't recognize it anyway. Strangely enough, in later life, whenever I've thought about what happened that day, it's not bitterness I've experienced but a sadness that so much young life was ruined, and in many cases ended because of an accident that probably could have been avoided if someone had taken the trouble to check movements.
>
> I was lucky, it taught me to value life. Those who were disabled or crippled for life after it, probably feel bitter about it, and who can blame them?[21]

Incidents where the aircraft was the victim are the hardest to quantify. This is also the hardest aspect of recognition for not only is the "target" very small and moving at great speed but it may be coming out of the sun. Psychological factors have an important bearing here: guns' crews who have been repeatedly bombed or strafed are more likely to fire first and worry about the niceties of recognition afterwards. The lack of friendly air cover, a situation in which the Royal Navy found itself for most of the early part of the war, often led to all aircraft being assumed to be hostile. This attitude is nicely shown in the cover photograph of this book and well illustrated in this recollection by Commander V. A. Wight-Boycott RN of the destroyer HMS *Ilex* in 1943:

> We sighted a strange aircraft. I gave the order to the Oerlikons to open fire, but as I did so, the plane turned at right-angles to us so we could see the markings, which were British. I immediately pressed the cease-fire gongs, but to my horror, almost every gun in the ship opened up. Even the two 4.7-inch guns' crews, who were not closed up, came rushing up and got a round away. Having tasted blood they took a lot of stopping.[22]

The most common reason for ships firing on their own aircraft is failure of recognition. Secondary factors are strain and carelessness caused by repeated air attacks with little or no friendly air cover and poor organization whereby there is insufficient separation between formations of aircraft and naval forces. On 22 August, 1940, the Italian submarine *Iride* was lying alongside the depot ship *Monte Gargano* with the torpedo boat *Calipso* in company, off Jezirat el Marakeb in the Bay of Bomba on the North African coast. The submarine was making final preparations for a "human-torpedo" attack on the British fleet at Alexandria. That morning they were attacked by three Swordfish aircraft from 824 Squadron who had been disemarked from HMS *Eagle* and both the *Iride* and the *Monte Gargano* were sunk. The *Calipso* was trying to organize some kind of rescue for those still trapped in the submarine when an unidentified aircraft was sighted heading into the Bay. Without so much as a challenge the aircraft was fired on and turned away, trailing smoke. It was, in fact, an Italian plane making a routine approach to a nearby airfield – which it eventually reached. The Italians investigated the incident and noted that the *Calipso's* gunners were "understandably sensitive seamen".

It was in similar circumstances that two Fulmar aircraft were shot down, one by HMS *Prince of Wales* and the other by HMS *Rodney* on 27 September, 1941, during the passage of an eastbound convoy to Malta, operation *Halberd*. In the confused circumstances of repeated air attacks, Italian and British aircraft were milling

65

about together and it was inevitable that some mistakes in identi-fication should occur.

The ordeal suffered by the Royal Navy in the Eastern Mediterranean at the hands of the *Luftwaffe* in the spring of 1941 is well known. Air attacks were frequent and claimed a heavy toll of ships sunk and damaged: friendly air cover was virtually non-existent. After the Germans launched their airborne assault on Crete, it was decided to attempt to operate Hurricane fighter air-craft of the RAF from Heraklion where a strip had been cleared and levelled. Twelve aircraft were sent from Eygpt in two flights of six. The first flight were fired on by the main body of the Mediterranean Fleet as they approached Crete: two were shot down, three returned to Eygpt and only one made it to Heraklion. By the time the second flight set off order had been restored, the fleet had been warned and all six arrived. Failure of recognition was undoubtedly the cause in this case, compounded by the extreme strain under which the guns' crews were suffering having been under continual air attack.

The various large-scale amphibious operations carried out by the allies in the Second World War involved the co-ordinated use of aircraft, either paratroop-carrying or glider-towing, and ships, carrying and escorting the main assault force and its equipment. Routes were carefully worked out to separate air-craft and ships.

However, in the airborne landings over Sicily things went ter-ribly wrong. On the night of 10/11 July men of the 504 Parachute Infantry Regiment of the 82 Airborne Division US Army boarded 144 C-47 Skytrain transports in North Africa. Their route to the drop zone around the airfield of Gela was laid out over a deserted stretch of coastline between the sectors occupied by the Western Task Force (WTF) and Eastern Task Force (ETF). The route was announced to WTF and ETF commanders and they were warned to stay clear of the airborne "corridor". For a number of reasons, including bad navigation and heavy flak, many of the aircraft took a shorter route over the Western Task Force's area. It was doubly unfortunate that the C-47s arrived over the WTF at the same time and from the same direction as a German air raid. Twenty-three of the transports were shot down and thirty-seven others badly damaged. Ninety-seven officers and men were killed and 400 wounded.

Forty-eight hours later, on the night of 13/14 July, the incident was repeated involving troops of the British 1st Airborne Division who were jumping over Catania. On this occasion the decision to proceed with the operation was taken too late for the details to be properly distributed to all ships and commands in the area. This led to the aircraft flying over an Allied convoy near Augusta, who had not been told of the operation, and a number of aircraft were shot down. In his report on the incident the Commander in Chief, Admiral Sir Andrew Cunningham, noted that the problem arose when military aircraft were routed to fufil tactical requirements after the main assault, and when communications were grossly overloaded. He emphasized, however, that friendly aircraft **must** keep clear of shipping formations at night.

In the planning for operation *Overlord,* the invasion of NW Europe, considerable effort was taken to ensure that there was no repeat of this incident. In practice, however, it proved impossible for the naval force commanders to persuade the air staffs to part with all the relevant information before the ships sailed. As the Staff History succinctly commented, "Lack of information resulted in foreseen situation".

At dusk on 6 June orders were given to lay a smoke screen over the invasion anchorage in anticipation of a dusk air attack which developed shortly afterwards. The attack occurred immediately before the arrival of the last re-supply mission by transport aircraft of 46 Group for the day. In the confusion light AA guns ashore opened fire, followed by AA fire from ships and landing craft in the anchorage despite repeated signals to cease fire. On board HMS *Scylla,* the flagship of the Eastern Task Force, commanded by Vice Admiral Sir Philip Vian, observers saw a Ju-88 passing down the ship's side at masthead height followed by two C-47s at 1,000 feet. Five aircraft were lost and fourteen damaged. Moreover, there was considerable dislocation as a result of the firing, so that only twenty tons of the 116 tons despatched were collected. Vian made urgent representations to Admiral Sir Bertram Ramsay, the naval CinC for *Overlord* (and knowing Vian's nature as a no-nonsense fighting admiral who cared little for politeness, those "represenations" would have been couched in no uncertain terms) and as a result airborne operations of this nature were confined to daylight hours.

Aircraft recognition was difficult enough for naval gunners: for merchant seamen it was even harder. This is no reflection on their skills, rather the fact that they suddenly had to absorb new skills in a tearing hurry. The introduction of the escort carrier provided convoys with their own organic air cover. The problem of aircraft identification for merchant seamen suddenly became more acute. On the Atlantic route where the air threat was non-existent once out of range of land-based aircraft, the risk of aircraft being fired on by the convoy was further reduced by manoeuvring the carrier at some distance from the convoy with her own escorts. However, on the Arctic route to the North Russian ports of Murmansk and Archangel the situation was very different. Before escort carriers became available, the convoys were allocated a CAM[23] with its single hurricane fighter perched on a catapult above the bows. Convoy PQ. 15 was the first convoy to be allocated a CAM ship (*Empire Morn*) and thereafter it became standard. The CAM ship for the next convoy, PQ. 16, was *Empire Lawrence*. On 25 May, 1942, the convoy was attacked by a mixed force of He-111s and Ju-88s from III/KG26 and III/KG30. The Hurricane fighter, flown by Pilot Officer A. J. Hay RAF, was flown and shot down one He-111 and damaged another before being shot down by gunfire from the American merchant ship *Carlton*. Fortunately, Hay was unharmed and rescued by the destroyer HMS *Volunteer*.

PQ. 18 was the first convoy to be accompanied by an escort carrier and thereafter nearly every convoy going to Russia possessed its organic air cover. It would have been ideal for the carrier to operate with her own escort away from the convoy but there were not enough escorts. So the carriers had to operate within a "box" in the centre of the convoy. During the winter of 1944/45 foul weather had reduced the tempo of *Luftwaffe* operations against Arctic convoys, but in February, 1945, convoy JW. 64 (and the return convoy RA. 64) endured the full Arctic repertoire of appalling weather and frequent air and submarine attacks. Against air attacks the convoy put up a large anti-aircraft artillery barrage, designed to intimidate an attacking pilot as much as to shoot his aircraft down. During this barrage, the carriers had to launch and recover their aircraft in the middle of an air battle. Casualties were inevitable:

> The two carriers were operating in their box in the centre rear of the convoy and the guns' crews joined in with enthusiasm firing at everything and anything in sight. Unfortunately as some of the Wildcats came in to land, two of *Campania's* fighters were shot down by the convoy's own anti-aircraft gunfire. One pilot was saved.[24]

Orders were subsequently issued that all "friendly" aircraft should only approach the convoy from astern and that the single engine F4F Wildcat fighters should do so with their undercarriage down. Additionally aircrew not required for flying duties were stationed at *Nairana's* gun positions to assist the gunners in identification of friendly aircraft. In his report Rear Admiral Rhoderick McGrigor, the escort commander, admitted that fire discipline was very poor among both the merchant ships and escorts which:

> showed a quite inexcusable lack of fire discipline even taking into account the bad visibility, low cloud and pace of events. There is little resemblance between a Ju. 88 and a Wildcat and none with a Swordfish.[25]

However, the aircrew could be said to have had their revenge some days later when an armourer working on a Wildcat's .50 calibre armament in the hangar accidently touched the firing button. Unusually, the weapon was armed and a spray of bullets went up through *Nairana's* flight deck causing consternation in a gunners' mess nearby. Fortunately no one was injured.

In the Far East theatre, damage from "friendly" AA fire increased significantly after the Japanese began to employ dedicated suicide aircraft, *Kamikazes*. There was nothing new about the Japanese fighting to the bitter end or killing themselves to avoid capture: that was all part of the Japanese military code. However, as the war went against them in the Pacific, their commanders resorted to ever more desperate means to stop the Americans. One

69

such means was organized suicide attacks which were first employed in October, 1944, during the Battle for Leyte Gulf. In the Okinawa campaign (March-June, 1945) the Japanese lost over 1900 aircraft shot down in massed suicide attacks.[26]

Those on the receiving end of a *Kamikaze* attack found it an awesome and terrifying experience. Both British and American personnel who experienced suicide attacks recalled that they felt that the pilot was aiming for them *individually.* Massed air attacks were nothing new to the Allies in the Second World War but nothing had prepared them for the inhuman, almost robotic way in which the Japanese just kept on coming. Moreover AA fire was surprisingly ineffective: 2 pdr, 20mm and 40mm gunfire merely knocked bits off the aircraft, the remnants of which continued on their fatal course. It took a hit from a 3-inch or even a 5-inch AA gun to shoot one down. The result was that tremendous AA barrages were put up during *Kamikaze* attacks. Not all this gunfire was co-ordinated, much of it going astray. On 18 March, 1945, the carrier USS *Enterprise* was damaged by AA fire which made it impossible for her to launch or recover aircraft. Throughout the Okinawa Campaign another twelve ships were damaged by AA fire. A small number perhaps, when compared to the 164 damaged by *Kamikaze* but it was still another twelve ships using the already strained repair facilities.

The general rules protecting carrier aircraft from "friendly" AA fire were severely tested during *Kamikaze* attacks. On 6 April, 1945, the aircraft carrier HMS *Illustrious* was damaged by a *Kamikaze* during strikes on Sakashima Gunto, Japanese-held islands to the west of Okinawa which were being used as staging points for aircraft reinforcements from the Japanese air force in China. . The ship's gunners were naturally under some strain since this was their first exposure to this sort of attack and, when a second attack developed in the evening, two planes were seen to be diving on *Illustrious.* Both were taken under fire and were shot down. The first was a Judy, a D4Y *Suisei* single-engine dive bomber often used as a suicide weapon, but the second was a Seafire which was chasing the Japanese aircraft. The pilot of the aircraft was killed.

A similar incident occurred on 4 May, 1945, during the British Pacific Fleet's second series of strikes against Sakashima Gunto. The battleships were directed to carry out a shore bombardment and in their absence the *Kamikazes* struck. The aircraft carriers *Formidable* and *Indomitable* were both hit, and thereafter there were numerous aircraft alerts throughout the rest of the day. Lieutenant Geoffrey Brooke was *Formidable's* Flight Deck Fire and Crash Officer and since, after the *Kamikaze* strike there were no flying operations while the clearing up was in progress, he strapped himself into a 20mm Oerlikon position taking the place of a gunner who had been killed:

> During a stand-to a lone fighter came in sight on the port beam almost out of the sun and made for us in a shallow dive. I gave him a long burst and had the immense satisfaction of seeing him dip suddenly and splash into the sea. Easing the leather straps off my shoulders, I locked the gun stationary and stepped down from its platform with a sense of deep satisfaction. Not only was it a good effort, but I had almost certainly saved the ship considerable damage.
>
> The Gunnery Officer's broadcast system clicked on to introduce the usual background hum, and I stopped to listen. Dan Duff's driest tone drained the colour from my face – "That was one of ours". I have had some shocks in my naval life but for unmitigated horror this was probably the worst.[27]

The aircraft was a damaged Hellcat returning to *Formidable*. Since it did not approach the carrier on a designated safe path, Brooke was justified in firing. Fortunately the pilot was picked up by HMS *Undaunted* none the worse for his ordeal.

One unwelcome side effect of the terrific anti-aircraft barrages put up by convoys or other naval formations was that safety arcs of fire were often ignored and that a merchant ship in the next column received a spray of AA fire intended for an aircraft. This was also the case in exercises as the following humorous exchange of signals between the aircraft carrier HMS *Indomitable* and the battleship HMS *Howe* shows. At the time the exchange took place both ships were part of TF. 57, supporting the American Fifth Fleet off Okinawa. After an AA practice *Indomitable* signalled:

> One of my Aircraft Handling Party was struck painlessly on the buttock by a fragment of shell fired during Serial 5.

To which the battleship replied:

> Your 0950. Please convey my regrets to the rating and ask him to turn the other cheek.

# CHAPTER SIX

## *Ships vs Submarines*

Tell those Bastards to stop firing!

*Commanding Officer of HM Submarine* Trusty *on being shelled by a large portion of the Home Fleet, 9 March, 1945.*

The submarine was the international pariah of both World Wars. Submarines were the victims of more friendly fire incidents than any other type of warship, so much so that the next four chapters are devoted to submarine victims of various forms of attack. When proceeding in waters frequented by friendly ships, submarines would have an escort, usually a trawler or converted yacht or some such vessel. The purpose of the escort was to protect the submarine from the attentions of her own side, the escort being larger and hus more easily seen. The value of the escort is shown in the ordeal of the American submarine USS *Thresher* which was shelled and bombed by her own side in December,1941, after she had detached her escort.

USS *Thresher* was returning to Pearl Harbor from a forty-eight-day training patrol off Midway, when on 7 December, 1941, she received the message: "Air raid Pearl Harbor This is no drill". *Thresher* had an escort, the destroyer USS *Litchfield*. Under the stress of the situation *Thresher's* Commanding Officer (who intended to remain dived for most of the day anyway) released *Litchfield* in order that she might join a task group forming up to search for the Japanese carriers. However, someone on the staff at Pearl Harbor was evidently thinking about the situation, for, just

73

before she dived, *Thresher* received a signal ordering that under no circumstances was she to detach her escort. Too late – *Litchfield* had gone but another rendezvous was arranged.

At the rendezvous position *Thresher* sighted another destroyer through the periscope which was not *Litchfield* but which *Thresher's* Commanding Officer thought had been sent in her place. However, when *Thresher* surfaced she was greeted with a hail of gunfire: the destroyer was not waiting for any submarine and had taken *Thresher* to be a Japanese boat – an understandable error in view of the fact that Japanese submarines were known to have been off Pearl Harbor the previous evening. *Thresher* dived quickly and remained dived overnight, only to be attacked by an American aircraft on surfacing the next morning. *Thresher* remained dived until the destroyer USS *Thornton* was sent out to bring her in, and it was not until late afternoon on 8 December that she finally secured alongside the depot ship.

Why were submarines so at risk? Firstly and most obviously, one submarine looks very much like another, especially when viewed from some distance away and even more so when seas were washing over the casing leaving the conning tower as the only point of reference. Secondly, if a surface ship detected a dived submarine and there was any doubt about the submarine's identity, it was best to depth-charge first rather than risk being added to the Roll of Honour. Lastly, and from a peculiarly British perspective, the U-boat was **the** enemy. This was the weapon which the Germans had used in two world wars with the intention of starving Britain into surrender. In his classic novel about the Battle of the Atlantic, *The Cruel Sea*, Nicholas Monsarrat expressed this feeling perfectly when the crew of his fictional corvette HMS *Compass Rose* (which has since passed into the naval literature as the archetypal Atlantic heroine) depth-charge a U-boat to the surface:

> it was odd and infinitely disgusting, suddenly to see this
> wicked object, this loathsome cause of a hundred nights
> of fear and disaster, so close to them, so innocently
> exposed. It was like seeing a criminal who had outraged
> honour and society, and had long been shunned, taking
> his ease at one's fireside. . . . They were people from

another and infinitely abhorrent world – not just Germans, but U-boat Germans, doubly revolting.[1]

With a submarine in his sights and a DSO[2] in his imagination, any Royal Navy commanding officer, or indeed the commanding officer of any surface ship, would shoot first when confronted with an unknown submarine and ask questions later.

This attitude of "shoot first"(or in this case "ram first") lay behind the loss of the British submarine *Umpire* in July, 1941. *Umpire* (Lt Cdr M. R. G. Wingfield RN) was one of two U-class submarines to be built by the Royal Dockyard at Chatham. On completion she was sent "north-about" to the Clyde to begin trials and work-up with the Third Submarine Flotilla at Dunoon. Accordingly she joined the north-bound East Coast convoy EC4, though she was not declared as part of the escort. When the convoy was passing Aldeburgh a lone He-111 attacked the leading ships and *Umpire* performed her first dive at sea. When the attack was over *Umpire* returned to the surface but soon her port engine began to give trouble and she started to fall behind the convoy. Wingfield reported his predicament to the Convoy Commodore and a Motor Launch (ML) was ordered to stand by, but lost contact with her charge almost immediately.

Shortly after midnight convoy EC4 was due to pass the southbound FS44. Both convoys were using the same swept channel through the minefields and it was the procedure for convoys to keep to the right side of the channel so that they would pass each other port side to port side. However, Wingfield was surprised to see that the convoys had passed starboard to starboard as directly ahead of him he could see the blacked-out silhouettes of the leading merchant ships of the convoy. The usual course of action would be to alter course to starboard but this would have meant *Umpire* crossing the path of the leading merchant ships of the convoy. Instead Wingfield altered course to port in the hope that the convoy would pass down his starboard side without incident.

The merchant ships did not see the low-lying submarine, but a trawler, the *Peter Hendriks,* part of the convoy escort, did. Wingfield saw the trawler alter course toward him but could not go to starboard, the accepted procedure under these circumstances,

75

because his way was blocked by the leading ships of the convoy. Instead, Wingfield went to port but the trawler followed him round and crashed into the submarine's starboard side midway between the bow and the conning tower. It is interesting to note at this stage that no challenge was offered by the trawler and no attempt was made by *Umpire* to identify herself.

The submarine lurched to port and for a few seconds the two vessels were locked together. Wingfield clutched at the trawler's side and shouted, "You bloody bastard, you've sunk a British submarine," before he, the two lookouts and Lieutenant Tony Godden, the navigating officer, were swept off the bridge as *Umpire* sank beneath them. Of these four, only Wingfield was later picked up. By a stroke of luck the conning tower hatch slammed shut as *Umpire* sank and thus the control room was not flooded.

She settled with her bows on the bottom at 80°. All attempts at blowing the submarine to the surface using HP air failed, so those left alive inside would have to escape. There were two groups of survivors: twenty were gathered in the engine room and were attempting to escape via the engine room hatch, while crammed into the narrow conning tower were Lieutenant Peter Bannister, the first lieutenant, Sub-Lieutenant Edward Young, the Third Hand, and two ratings. With four men in the conning tower it was a tight squeeze:

> Peter at the top of the ladder with his head jammed up against the upper hatch, the AB half way up the ladder with his bottom wedged against the side of the tower leaving just room for me and the ERA[3] at the foot of the tower, with our feet on the edge of the lower hatch opening. The ERA was in a bad way, vomiting continuously and hardly able to stand.[4]

The lower lid was shut and an attempt made to lift the upper lid, but the sea pressure was too great. However, inside the unflooded section of *Umpire* the air pressure had been steadily rising owing to the continual inrush of water. Young carefully lifted the lower lid and heard the sound of air forcing its way into the tower. On the next attempt the upper hatch moved slightly and Bannister suggested waiting until more pressure built up. However, Young and the AB, the ERA having "reached the point in his sickness when he wanted to die more than anything else", argued to go immediately on the grounds that they could smell chlorine gas. Bannister pushed hard on the upper lid and up went the four in a bubble of air. Young was picked up by a motor launch but none of his companions in this escape survived.

The other group of survivors, twenty in all, were gathered in the engine room under the leadership of Chief ERA George Killen. Killen organized a textbook escape through the engine room hatch using the Davis Submarine Escape Apparatus (DSEA). The escape was accomplished with the loss of only two of the twenty trapped men. The first man out was CERA George Killen who thought it would be advisable to check that the way to the surface was clear and that the hatchway was not blocked by debris. He donned a DSEA set, then made his way onto the casing, "walked about a bit", as he put it, and then re-entered the engine room to supervise the escape of the rest. Killen was the last man out of the boat. For this feat of cold blooded courage Killen was awarded the BEM,[5] though many believe that he deserved a higher honour. Two officers and fourteen ratings were all that survived the loss of *Umpire* out of a ship's company of four officers and thirty-four ratings.

One of the Admiralty's more bizarre ideas during the Second World War was to employ submarines as convoy escorts in the North Atlantic. For one thing it was a waste of an asset to have a submarine trundling across the ocean with an eight knot convoy when it could have been offensively employed against the enemy, while for another it placed the submarine in great danger of attack from the convoy's escort: the main threat to the convoys was, after all, the U-boat. The North Atlantic Escort Force was based on the submarine depot ship HMS *Forth* at Halifax, Nova Scotia and consisted of the submarines *Taku, Tribune, Thunderbolt, Talisman* and the French *Surcouf.* Fortunately the Admiralty did not persist with this policy for long, but not before one of the submarines was shelled by an Armed Merchant Cruiser.

In February, 1941, the British submarine HMS *Thunderbolt* (Lieutenant Commander C. B. Crouch RN) was ordered to Halifax to join the North Atlantic Escort Force. On 24 February she was headed westwards, having parted company with her escort, the corvette HMS *Asphodel*. Lieutenant John Stevens was her first lieutenant:

> A week after we sailed, I was OOW on the bridge for the morning watch. The weather and visibility were good, with a moderate swell and low grey cloud. Searching the horizon through powerful binoculars, I sighted the mast and funnel of a hull-down ship. I ordered "diving stations" and called for the captain to come up to the bridge. Our courses were now converging, and as she drew nearer, she was identified as a large grey-painted passenger ship. As there had been no information about any friendly forces in the area we assumed her to be a German or Italian vessel. The torpedo tubes were brought to the ready and when we were three miles away from her Crouch ordered the signalman to make the challenge.
>
> The signalman spelt out the group of letters using a large Aldis lamp but there was no reply. Instead she swung round under full helm and opened fire on us with her main battery. The shell splashes came alarmingly close and Crouch cleared the bridge and pressed the diving klaxon.[6]

The ship was the British armed merchant cruiser *Canton* and her fire was accurate: *Thunderbolt* was lucky to get away unscathed. But why had *Canton* opened fire when the submarine had given the challenge? The problem was that *Thunderbolt* had not made the challenge then in force:

> the problem with these long Atlantic voyages was that routine relaxed and everyone got a little careless. The signalman hadn't checked the correct challenge for the day, which is why we were fired on.[7]

78

Stevens was right. A few days later, as a result of information obtained from reading German naval signals, *Thunderbolt* was given a position from which she could intercept the German *U-557*. The interception was made but poor torpedo drill, by men who had not been fully on their mettle, meant that the opportunity of sinking a U-boat was wasted.

Three days later in the Irish Sea, the Dutch submarines *O. 21* and *O. 23* were on passage to Gibraltar from the Clyde. Their escort was the Free-French minesweeping sloop *La Moquese*. On the evening of 26 February the three ships put into Holyhead to take on fresh provisions but sailed that evening. Throughout the night the weather worsened and *La Moquese's* station-keeping became so irregular that the Commanding Officer of *O. 23* ( Lt Cdr G. B. M. Van Erkel RNethN) ordered her to take station astern of him – a most unusual arrangement given that under normal circumstances it was the surface escort (which was the more visible ship) which was responsible for navigation, and thus took the lead.

At 1600 on the next day, 27 February, the ships were abreast of the Smalls Light and at 1733 they encountered the steamship *Losada* in very poor visibility. *Losada* opened fire on the submarines since she evidently did not see the surface escort. The two Dutch submarines turned away to port in order to give *La Moquese* the chance to come up and identify the submarines as friendly, but when one shell fell fifty yards from *O. 23* Van Erkel decided to dive, as did *O. 21*. After about ten minutes *La Moquese* appeared and since the *Losada* was not in sight any more, *O. 23* surfaced. As she did so three loud explosions were heard close by, so *O. 23* remained dived for a further 20 minutes before surfacing. On asking *La Moquese* what had happened, Van Erkel was told that O. 21 had surfaced very close to *La Moquese,* had been taken for a U-boat and attacked. No damage was done and the ships proceeded toward the Bristol Channel, although this time *La Moquese* was kept in front where she was obviously less of a menace.

The British Liaison Officer (BNLO) in *La Moquese*, Lieutenant J. B. Selwyn RNR, felt bound to submit his own report on the incident to the Captain of the 3rd Submarine Flotilla, which he marked as "a personal one and no one on board has seen it or is aware of its contents".[8] In his report Selwyn stated that after being ordered to take station astern of the submarines, *La Moquese* was unable to keep up and requested a reduction in speed of two knots. The signal was acknowledged by the nearer submarine and the two submarines could be seen communicating by light, so those on *La Moquese*'s bridge thought that the message was being passed to *O. 23*. However, no reduction was apparent and the two submarines gradually drew ahead and were lost to sight. Selwyn then went below but was called to the bridge at 1745. Just as he reached the bridge a periscope was sighted on the port bow. *La Moquese* altered course and when abeam of the periscope three depth charges were dropped:

> one from the port thrower (which naturally overshot the target), and two from the racks aft. All three were set to 250°, the officer concerned told me afterwards that he did not use a smaller setting because of the slow speed we were doing (6 knots) and because he thought the submarine was going to crash dive. The 37mm fired one round at the periscope but missed. The order was given to fire but the gun did not go off. The periscope began to rise and the 3-inch gun was trained on it ready to fire. Then by a stroke of good fortune, as the submarine was rising, a big trough beneath the waves enabled us to get a glimpse of the upper part of the Dutch ensign. The order was immediately given not to fire.[9]

*O. 21* then surfaced and gave the correct recognition signal. There followed an exchange of signals by Aldis lamp which would be quite funny were it not for the fact that a serious incident had just been averted:

| | |
|---|---|
| *La M*: | Are you in trouble? |
| *O. 21*: | I don't think so. |
| *La M*: | If you are going to do things like that you should warn us.[10] |

Selwyn then suggested that *La Moquese* assume command of the formation as "the existing arrangements were becoming dangerously chaotic"[11] and the ships proceeded. There are considerable variances in the reports of this incident with the Commanding Officer of *O. 23* maintaining that he was in command while the Commanding Officer of *La Moquese* claiming the opposite. The Dutch do not mention *La Moquese*'s request to reduce speed and the French claim not to have heard the gunfire from the *Losada*. National pride was evidently very much at stake.

The incident was investigated by the Captain, Third Submarine Flotilla, Captain H. M. C. Ionides RN, who considered the Commanding Officer of *O. 23* to have been at fault for i) in not having stationed the submarines astern of *La Moquese*, ii) in allowing *La Moquese* to fall behind, iii) having dived, in not surfacing before *La Moquese* was in sight and iv) for not having fired the submerged recognition signal. *La Moquese* did not escape censure either. Ionides considered that although her Commanding Officer was in an invidious position, he was justified in attacking. Ionides concluded that orders be issued to the effect that submarines were always to be stationed astern of their escorts who were to be responsible for navigation.

However, the Free French naval authorities were much stricter in their treatment of *La Moquese*'s Commanding Officer. After considering various omissions and inadequacies in his report, Vice-Admiral Auboyneau, Senior Free French Naval Officer, Clyde, concluded that:

> If the submarine had really been an enemy, the Commanding Officer of *La Moquese* should be severely censured – if not relieved of his command – for not having sunk her in such favourable circumstances. In effect, his mistakes are many and serious:
> i)    bad regulation of the depth charges
> ii)   not having in the presence of the enemy gone to full speed in an endeavour to ram and sink the submarine
> iii)  not having opened fire on the submarine with all armament.[12]

It seems that the lessons from this incident were not learned, for two years later one officer and several ratings were wounded on board the French submarine *La Vestale* which was rammed by HMS *Wishart* (Commander H.G. Scott RN) off the coast of Algiers in May, 1943. The French submarine was on passage from Oran to Algiers and was running on the surface with a British ML as the escort – the ML was disposed astern of the submarine. *Wishart* was escorting a damaged merchant ship to Oran and had not been informed that *La Vestale* would be in the area. On sighting the sub-marine *Wishart* opened fire and turned to ram. Fortunately the submarine was able to identify herself in good time to prevent total destruction but there were a number of casualties. *Wishart* sustained enough damage to warrant docking in Oran.

Navigational error was a prime factor in many of these incidents. On 2 May, 1942, the Polish submarine ORP *Jastrazb* (Lt Cdr B. S. Romanowski) was sunk by the Norwegian destroyer *St Albans* (Commander S.V. Storeheil) and HMS *Seagull* (Lt Cdr J. Pollock RN). *Jastrazb* was an American S class submarine, the *S-25*, and had been built in 1923. By 1941 she was old and unsuitable for frontline service. Doubtless, however, the American government was quite prepared to sell her to Poles who had plenty of cash with which to buy American equipment and were desperate to be in the thick of the war against Germany. She was formally commissioned into the Polish Navy in November, 1941, at the submarine base at New London, Connecticut. After a refit at Blyth she sailed for his first and only patrol on 22 April, 1942, in an area 180 miles NW of Altenfjord in Northern Norway.

Romanowski and his crew endured a week of bad weather and mechanical difficulties. Then at 1600 on 2 May he sighted a U-boat running on the surface and prepared to attack. His attempt, however, was plagued with mechanical problems, and Roman-owski reluctantly had to abandon the attack. At about 1945 *Jastrazb* picked up the noise of approaching engines on her hydrophones and after a while Romanowski could see ships through his periscope. After a quick look at his recognition book, he identified them as friendly and ordered the release of smoke candles to avoid being attacked. The smoke candles were fired from a 3-inch underwater "gun" built into the submarine's pressure hull and ignited on reaching the surface. The signals were not seen by the two approaching ships which delivered a devastatingly accurate depth charge attack. The pressure hull was fractured in a number of places and water poured into the hull, contaminating the batteries which began to give out chlorine gas. Romanowski had no choice but to bring *Jastrazb* to the surface.

*Jastrazb*'s assailants were the Norwegian destroyer *St Albans* and the minesweeper HMS *Seagull*: both were part of the escort for convoy PQ. 15 heading for the Soviet port of Murmansk. They were steaming on the convoy's port bow – the opposite side of the convoy to where a British submarine might be expected – when they gained a solid Asdic contact and attacked it with depth charges in position 73° 30'N, 17° 35'E. The smoke candles fired by Jastrazb were not seen by either ship before the depth charges were fired.

*Jastrazb* surfaced between the two ships but with her bows pointed toward *St Albans* so that her pendant number, P. 551, was not visible. Both ships opened fire on the submarine with machine guns and *St Albans* also brought her 3-inch gun into action. Romanowski had been first onto the conning tower together with his British liaison officer and two Royal Navy signal ratings. The two ratings, were killed instantly, together with three Polish ratings, and six of her crew were wounded, including Romanowski, before *Seagull* recognized the pendant number and both ships ceased fire. Boats were launched to offer assistance but it was clear that *Jastrazb* was beyond salvage. The survivors were taken on board HMS *Seagull* (Romanowski even managed to bring all his Confidential Books with him – no mean feat!) before being transferred to the cruiser HMS *London*. While her crew were clamouring to go back to the war in a new submarine, *Jastrazb* was sunk by 4-inch gunfire from HMS *Seagull*. The most seriously wounded of *Jastrazb*'s crew were landed in Murmansk and treated in local hospitals which were not, contrary to much of what has been written about them[13], the dreadful places they have been made out to be. The most serious case was that of the British naval liaison officer, Sub-Lieutenant Maurice Hanbury RNVR, whose hand had been smashed by a bullet and who had a severe compound fracture of the leg, also caused by a bullet wound. Hanbury needed specialist orthopaedic treatment unavailable in Murmansk and it was decided to bring him back to England in the cruiser HMS *Trinidad*. He had suffered enough at the hands of his own side but was to have to endure one more sinking when *Trinidad* was bombed and sunk by the *Luftwaffe* on 14 May, 1942, before he could get the treatment he so urgently needed.

What had gone wrong? In theory the course of PQ. 15 should have taken the convoy well to the north of the submarine's patrol area. However, owing to heavy ice, the convoy had altered course to the south at 0945 that morning and was steaming diagonally across the submarine's intended track. On the other hand *Jastrazb* was hopelessly out of position, by as much as 100 miles to the north-east of his area. At the Enquiry into her loss, held in HMS *Forth*, her navigating officer said that he had been unable to take a sight of the sun or stars for five days, and had been navigating entirely by dead reckoning. His notes were examined and it was found that the allowances he had made for currents and tidal sets were accurate but that it was practically impossible for him to navigate properly since *Jastrazb* was not fitted with a bottom log nor was there any accurate method of checking engine revolutions. Under these circumstances an error of nearly 100 miles was understandable. The Enquiry concluded that *Jastrazb*'s loss was a misfortune of war, compounded by the difficulties of navigation in such high latitudes, and exonerated all three Commanding Officers.[14] Romanowski continued to serve in submarines and later commanded the submarine ORP *Dzik* in the Mediterranean with great distinction.

In June, 1942, the British submarine *P. 514* was rammed and sunk with the loss of all her crew by the minesweeper HMCS *Georgian*. *P. 514* was an old American submarine (ex-*R-19*) similar to *Jastrazb*, transferred to Britain and used for the training of escort groups on Canada's east coast. Under the command of Lieutenant Commander Richard Pain, and escorted by the corvette HMS *Primrose*, *P. 514* sailed on 20 June from Argentia bound for St John's in Newfoundland, 65 miles to the north. On the same day the minesweeper *Georgian* sailed from St John's to rendezvous with the coastal convoy CL-43 which she was to escort to Sydney, a small township on Cape Breton Island. The rendezvous was made at 1430 and passage began. *Georgian* had been informed that two

U-boats were believed to be operating off Cape Race but a signal informing the minesweeper that *P. 514* was at sea was not received.

In the early hours of 21 June *Georgian* picked up a faint but unmistakable diesel HE[15]. At the same time the HE from another convoy, SC-88, passing eight miles to the south of *Georgian,* was also picked up. *Georgian*, convoy SC-88 and *P-514* and her escort were all in the same area at the same time. At 0307 a darkened shape was seen crossing *Georgian*'s bows from starboard to port. No recognition procedures were carried out and *Georgian* rammed the submarine squarely amidships at full speed. When *Primrose* indicated the identity of the submarine, a search was begun for any survivors but none was found. In the inevitable investigation, it was found that *Georgian* had not received the signal warning of *P-514*'s presence and that under the circumstances, the minesweeper's Commanding Officer had acted correctly but with tragic results.

The American submarine USS *Seawolf*, a *Seadragon* class submarine built in 1939 , was one of the most distinguished American submarines serving in the Pacific. In fourteen patrols and under two Commanding Officers *Seawolf* had sunk 71,609 tons of Japanese shipping. Her fifteenth patrol, under the command of Lieutenant Commander A. L. Bontier USN, was a special operation delivering supplies and personnel to the east coast of Samar in the Philippines. Her operation coincided with a Seventh Fleet strike on the island of Morotai and in order to protect American submarines in the area, a submarine "sanctuary" had been established to the north of Morotai. On 2 October, 1944, Bontier reported to Commander Seventh Fleet that bad weather had set him back by 24 hours but that he was within the "sanctuary" where he was sighted by *Narwhal* on 3 October.

However, on 3 October the destroyer USS *Shelton* was torpedoed by the Japanese submarine *Ro-41* commanded by Lieutenant Commander M. Shiizuka IJN while screening a Seventh Fleet carrier task group. Good damage control saved the *Shelton* from sinking but she could not proceed with the task group so the USS *Rowell* was ordered to stand by her to render assistance.

Meanwhile the task group despatched anti-submarine patrols and at 1130 two TBM Avengers were launched from the USS

85

*Midway*. One of these aircraft sighted and bombed a submarine, marking the spot with a dye marker. The attack actually took place within the "sanctuary" but the aircrew were not briefed about this, or of the presence of friendly submarines in the area before taking off. The attack was signalled to the *Rowell* which headed for the spot at top speed. On reaching the area she began an Asdic search and gained contact at 1310. The destroyer then delivered five attacks using her Hedgehog ahead-throwing weapon and one using depth charges. After the first Hedgehog attack garbled transmissions were heard on SST but these were disregarded since *Rowell*'s Commanding Officer considered that the submarine was trying to "jam" his own Asdic. Another Hedgehog attack was delivered and four or five explosions were observed. Unlike a depth charge, Hedgehog projectiles were fitted with a contact fuze: the bomb had to strike something before it would explode. Debris was blown to the surface, including something which resembled a periscope.

*Seawolf* was never heard from again following her sighting by *Narwhal* and, as submarine command at Pearl Harbor began to fit the evidence together, the grim truth emerged. Four American submarines, including *Seawolf*, were in the area when *Shelton* was torpedoed. However, the position given by *Seawolf* in her signal of 2 October reporting herself 24 hours behind schedule was only thirty-two miles from the spot where *Shelton* was torpedoed. US forces in the area were not told of *Seawolf*'s presence, nor were the aircrew told of a submarine "sanctuary" then in force in which the bombing of submarines was prohibited.

The Enquiry into her loss concluded that *Seawolf* had been sunk either by the Avengers from *Midway* or by the *Rowell*, although they favoured the latter. The SST transmissions heard by *Rowell* were later identified as the submarine trying to establish contact with the destroyer. The atmosphere in *Seawolf*'s Asdic room as the operators frantically tried to make contact using the SST as the destroyer bored in for another attack can only be imagined. The Enquiry noted that a number of individuals were guilty of errors of judgement but that no disciplinary action be taken. *Rowell*'s Commanding Officer was "subject to censure", but

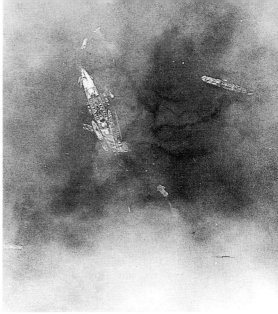

1. The swastika recognition mark on the fo'c'sle of the German cruiser *Prinz Eugen*. German ships only carried such markings in areas frequented by the *Luftwaffe*.

2. The Italian battleship *Littorio* at Taranto after the Fleet Air Arm attack of 11 November, 1940. The recognition stripes painted on the bow are clearly visible.

3. An impromptu aircraft recognition class in progress on the fo'c'sle of the battleship HMS *Rodney*. Models of aircraft are laid out on the deck. (*IWM A.15461*)

4. Seamen brushing up the recognition mark for display on the battleship *Tirpitz's* quarterdeck.

5. The British submarine *Sealion* arriving at Harwich in the winter of 1939/40. Note the White Ensign displayed on the front of the conning tower as a reminder to the RAF of the boat's nationality. (*RNSM*)

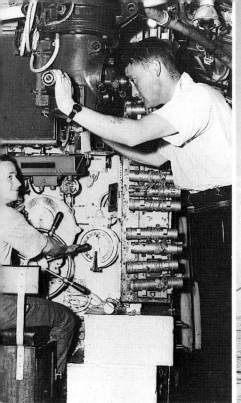

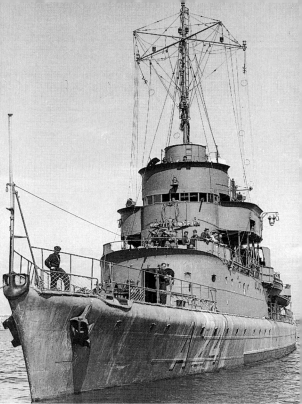

6. The commanding officer at the periscope of a British U-class submarine. Hanging on the bulkhead by the helmsman are the recognition signal flares. (*RNSM*)

7. The French Sloop *Commandant Duboc*, taken for a submarine by HMS *Legion* on the night of 23/24 October, 1941.

8. Admiral Sir Andrew Cunningham and Air Marshal Sir Charles Portal in an LCI(S) [Landing Craft Infantry (Small)] during the invasion of Normandy in June, 1944. Note the board on the bridge screen carrying details of the challenge/reply codes in force. (*IWM A.24203*)

9. The destroyer HMS *Campbell* which attacked HMS *Garth* on the night of 19/20 November, 1941.

10. The French destroyer *La Combattante* which sank *MTB.732* on the night of 27/28 May, 1944, after insufficient use had been made of IFF equipment. (*IWM A.13892*)

11. The destroyer *Lebrecht Maass* bombed and sunk by the *Luftwaffe* on 22 February, 1940.

12. HMS *Britomart* attacked and sunk by the RAF on a clear sunny day off Normandy in August, 1944. (*IWM FL.2980*)

13. HMS *Hussar* sunk with HMS *Britomart*. Two other minesweepers and two trawlers were damaged in the same attack. (*IWM FXL.4518*)

14. The twisted stern of HMS *Salamander* after a Typhoon rocket attack on 27 August, 1944.

15. Wing Commander J. Baldwin who led the RAF strike on the British minesweepers on 27 August, 1944. Though he believed the ships were friendly, he was ordered to go ahead by the shore controller. (*IWM CL.743*)

16. Arming a Typhoon with 60lb rockets at the B1 airfield in Normandy. These rockets did terrible damage to the thin hulls and superstructures of the minesweepers. (*IWM CL.1725*)

17. The American submarine *Seawolf*, sunk by the destroyer USS
*Rowell* on 3 October, 1944. (*US National Archives*)

18. The German *U-235* at Wilhelmshaven after her second
reconstruction. The wooden framework supports camouflage netting.
She was rammed and sunk by the torpedo boat *T.1* on 5 May, 1945.
(*UBA 1411/1/2*)

was not proceeded against after his errors were considered "due to over-zealousness to destroy an enemy".[16]

This incident was a clear case of the left hand not knowing what the right was up to. The Seventh Fleet task group disregarded all the provisions of the "sanctuary". *Seawolf*'s signal with her ammended position, although sent to Commander Seventh Fleet, was not passed on to the task group operating in the area. To add to the confusion a Japanese submarine had just demonstrated her presence in her area by torpedoing the *Shelton*. If the *Rowell* and the carrier task group had known that an American submarine was within 35 miles of the position where *Shelton* had been torpedoed, they would have proceeded with greater caution. At that time promulgation of Submarine Position Reports was not required by specific orders from higher authority; it was left to individual task group commanders to decide how much information to pass on about friendly submarines. After the loss of the *Seawolf*, their promulgation became mandatory. What of *Ro-41* and Lieutenant Commander Shiizuka? *Ro-41* returned to Japan unmolested. Five months later she was sunk by USS *Haggard* (DD555) 320 miles south east of Okinawa on 23 March, 1945.

One of the last such incidents took place on 9 March, 1945, and ended with the participants agreeing not to mention the incident further. No harm having been done, there seemed little point, but this illustrates the difficulty faced by the historian. On the morning of 9 March, 1945, the destroyer HMCS *Haida* (Cdr R. Welland RCN) and two other destroyers were returning to Scapa Flow from an anti-shipping strike off Norway when they passed close to the battleship HMS *Rodney* and her panoply of escorting cruisers and destroyers. The battleship was conducting AA practice and the three "strike" destroyers were ordered to join her screen. *Haida* took station on *Rodney*'s starboard beam. Visibility was only around three miles in heavy rain squalls so that the battleship was not visible to *Haida* all the time but kept looming in and out of the mist. The only ship in clear sight was the destroyer HMS *Zealous* which was 1.5 miles on *Haida*'s port bow. *Rodney* could be heard firing through the mist and shortly after 1000 a lookout on *Haida*'s bridge collapsed, having been shot through the neck by a stray

20mm Oerlikon round (the round rattled around the bridge and was retrieved by a signalman). That was the first incident of the day.

This event had barely subsided when our Chief Yeoman, Mackie, quietly but firmly pointed out to me a submarine periscope off our starboard quarter. It was about 800 yards off and quickly disappeared. I immediately turned hard to port, went full ahead and ordered a ten charge pattern set to 100° to be ready.

I assumed that the submarine was making a run at *Rodney* and the cruisers. The Chief Yeoman ordered his men to sound the attacking blasts on the siren, to flash the alarm to whoever was in sight and ordered the radio room to alert the fleet on voice radio. All of which was done in quick time. I steered the ship onto what I judged to be a good intercept course. The Asdic crew did not gain contact – the ship's speed was approaching 28 knots in a full heeled-over turn since we had all boilers on the line in our earlier hurry to get back into Scapa. I ordered firing and when the pattern was clear of the ship, turned hard to starboard and reduced to twelve knots in an attempt to get an Asdic contact for an accurate follow-up attack. Chief Mackie reported to me that the fleet had executed an emergency turn to port, and that the two nearest destroyers were joining for the hunt.

The submarine surfaced in the middle of the depth charge boil. My gunnery officer asked permission to open fire – the forward 4. 7" mountings were onto the submarine and I was appalled that they would open fire. I had instantly recognized the bow of the submarine as belonging to the British "T" class, and had my thumb bent far back as I pushed the "cease fire" gong. I was very familiar with the "T" class – we often exercised together, besides I was a specialist ASW officer, and was supposed to know these things. *Haida* did not fire a shot. The submarine was now lying stopped, 400 yards directly ahead, broadside on and badly down by the stern.[17]

By this stage the rest of the fleet had been well and truly stirred up. *Rodney* opened fire with her 6-inch armament and at least two of the cruisers followed suit (it was subsequently found that over 150 shells of 6-inch calibre or greater were fired by the cruisers and Rodney). *Haida* was broadcasting "cease fire" on every frequency and by any other medium but in the end Welland had to place his ship between the fleet and the submarine. At this stage a Polish destroyer ordered him to clear the range at once or be fired on! Eventually the gunfire subsided (even from the Poles) but it had been a very anxious few minutes.

Welland took *Haida* alongside the submarine and was pleasantly surprised and not a little embarrassed to find that it was HMS *Trusty* commanded by Lt P. H. May RN, an old friend of Welland's. "Tell the bastards to stop firing!" was May's greeting. *Haida* remained alongside *Trusty* for about an hour while the submarine made hasty repairs to the damage, before escorting her back to Scapa where they secured alongside each other. That evening both ships' companies "spliced the mainbrace" while there was a particularly lively wardroom party.

An informal enquiry was held onboard *Rodney* the next day. It transpired that the Duty Staff Officer in *Rodney* had given the order for *Haida* and her consorts to join the screen without informing anyone else on the staff. As a result details of the exercise were not passed to *Haida* and since she had been away on operations she had not received the routine signal about the exercise which was broadcast on the Administrative net two days beforehand. As a result none of the four "strike" destroyers were aware that *Trusty* was in the area. To complicate matters, a U-boat had been reported in the area which is why the fleet was zig-zagging. Welland continues:

> This known German threat enabled the trigger-fingered gunners in the cruisers and in *Rodney*'s secondary fire control tower to absolve themselves neatly from any responsibility in shelling the surfaced submarine. The gunners made the points that they were retiring from the scene, the visibility was poor, the range was close to 8,000 yards and they couldn't see the target clearly anyway. If the submarine was threat sufficient to warrant a

destroyer's depth charging, what was so wrong in shelling it? They had a point.

Commodore "D", who conducted the enquiry, publicly absolved *Haida* from any fault. He also congratulated us on the speed and accuracy of the attack, our timely warnings to the fleet, our blocking the range that stopped the gunfire. Not so fortunate were two of the Admiral's staff. They were reprimanded.[18]

*Trusty*'s version of events was that she had been observing the exercise from a distance and had watched *Haida* go right by without being detected – the submarine was end-on and thus presented a smaller target. May heard the increase in *Haida*'s speed and guessed that he had been seen and so dived to fifty feet to allow *Haida* to pass over before firing the recognition signal. The arrival of the ten-charge pattern came as a complete surprise. May later believed that the only thing which saved the boat was that the charges had been set for 100 feet. Had they been set any shallower, the submarine would have been sunk. As it was *Trusty* lost control and had to surface with a good deal of minor shock damage.

The incident was glossed over by both Welland and May, not out of any conspiracy but because it was adminstratively more convenient to do so:

> This incident was overlooked in official reporting both in the UK and in Canada. Why? Because Commodore "D" asked May and I (at dinner on the day of the enquiry) if our reporting rules demanded a report. May said that none of his crew were badly hurt; most of the damage could be fixed in Scapa and that he didn't much like writing reports anyway. I said that my immediate boss was the Commodore himself and that while I sent a monthly report to Canada, the omission of the *Trusty* incident would hardly be noticed.[19]

One month later *U-235*, a Type VIIC submarine, became the last submarine to be sunk by a surface ship from her own side in the Second World War. *U-235* was commissioned in December, 1942, and after trials and work-up with the 5 U-Flotilla in the Baltic, she returned to Germania Werft at Kiel for the usual repairs and alterations. While there, on 14 May, 1943, she was sunk in a daylight raid by the American 8th Air Force. Subsequently *U-235* was raised and re-commissioned on 30 October, 1943. For a while she was used as an instructional vessel with the 22 U-Flotilla but in April, 1945, she was transferred to the 31 U-Flotilla and employed on escort duties along the south coast of Norway. The circumstances attending the loss of *U-235* are very confused. The records of the operations section of the *Seekriegsleitung* contain one version while those of *Führer des U-bootes* in Norway contain another. Put together, the circumstances are as follows.

On 12 April, 1945, *U-235*, under the command of *Oberleutnant zur See der Reserve* Friedrich Huisgen, sailed from Kiel in company with *U-1272*, another Type VIIC boat commanded by *Oberleutnant zur See* Schatteburg. It was the intention of both Commanding Officers to proceed submerged during daylight hours, using their *schnorchels*, since the RAF had complete air superiority over the area they would be transiting. The next day, 13 April, a German convoy sailed from Denmark consisting of the ferry *Preussen* escorted by the torpedo boat *T. 17* (*Kapitän Leutnant* Hans Liermann) and a number of other escort vessels. Liermann had been told that U-boats were on passage to Norway and that they were likely to be in his area, but was not told the number of boats at sea nor the precise routes they would be taking.

At 0455 the *Preussen* reported a torpedo track to Liermann. The latter was aware that U-boats were in the area but was also aware that a British submarine (HMS *Varne*) had been reported off Korsfjord. To be on the safe side Liermann fired the correct recognition grenades but received no reply. At that very moment lookouts sighted a submarine surfacing close to *T. 17*. The boat was not identified but made a very rapid crash dive again. Liermann turned in to ram believing that, if the submarine were German, she would not have dived again. *T. 17* ran over the spot and dropped a full pattern of depth charges. Wreckage began to come up in the middle of the depth charge boil and the cheers of *T. 17*'s crew were abruptly stilled when amid all the gruesome detritus, bodies wearing familiar grey U-boat leathers were seen.

91

What had gone wrong? Had *U-235* identified the convoy as hostile and carried out an attack on the *Preussen?* The U-boat Commanding Officers had not been told about the convoy since convoy sailings were the responsbility of *Gruppe West,* while U-boat operations were the responsibility of *U-boot Führung.* The U-boats were proceeding in line ahead, dived and using their schnorchels, with *U-1272* in the lead. By chance their course led them straight across the path of the convoy. When Schatteburg realized that he was steaming into a German convoy he lowered his schnorchel and went deep. It was the wake made by the head of *U-1272*'s schnorchel which was seen by *Preussen* and identified as a torpedo track. Liermann in *T. 17* then performed the standard procedure in these circumstances which was to run down the track of the torpedo; as he did so *U-235* surfaced in front of him with the tragic results referred to. Perhaps *U-235* was coming to the surface to identify herself but saw that *T. 17* was too close and that a collision was imminent, so decided to dive instead. We shall never know. There was a brief enquiry held into her loss which concluded that U-boats should surface in the presence of friendly forces and be identified.

# CHAPTER SEVEN

## *Aircraft vs Submarines*

The risk of missing an enemy is preferable to the risk of sinking
one of ours.

*Commander H. C. Browne RN after an attack by an RAF Hampden
bomber on HMS Sceptre.*

Aircraft attacks on friendly submarines are the most numerous
friendly fire incidents. This survey has identified thirty-eight such
incidents (although the true total is probably a good deal higher)
which resulted in the definite sinking of five submarines (one British,
one French, one Italian and two Soviet) and the probable sinking of
another two submarines where the evidence is not conclusive.

In discussing the causes for such incidents Commander H. C.
Browne RN, a distinguished submarine Commanding Officer, put
the matter in a nutshell after a RAF Hampden had just depth-
charged HMS *Sceptre* in June, 1943:

> The causes of these incidents may be resolved into three
> groups, namely: negligence of RAF Staff Officers; care-
> lessness, casualness or stupidity of the aircrews and
> inefficient navigation.[1]

On passage to and from their patrol areas, submarines were protected by what was known as a Total Bombing Restriction Area.
This was defined in CB-03092 (1942) as an area where no submarines were to be attacked by day or night. Enemy submarines
were to be reported by radio. For additional safety the Total

93

Bombing Restriction Area was extended 20 miles either side of the submarine's track and a further 20 miles each side of the track would be added to compensate for navigational errors by the aircrew, making a total of 40 miles either side of track. Even these precautions were not sufficient to prevent attacks. As one British submariner, Lieutenant John Coote, the "Third Hand" of HMS *Untiring* put it:

> All the restrictions in the world didn't guarantee immunity from a keyed-up Wellington pilot dropping out of the overcast and seeing his first ever U-boat right in front of him with Distinguished Service Order written all over it.[2]

More than one British submarine Commanding Officer must have echoed the sentiments of the unknown submarine Commanding Officer who signalled, "My ETA (time) RAF permitting". Why were so many submarines attacked? Faulty navigation and poor recognition skills are two reasons. The nature of the submarine as Britain's main threat in the Atlantic and Home Waters is another. A fourth factor is the boredom encountered during aircraft anti-submarine patrols. A crew could go for months without seeing so much as the "feather" thrown up by a periscope. Suddenly a submarine would appear and, in the excitement of the moment, recognition drills were sometimes quickly forgotten.

Most incidents concerned British or American submarines. This is not solely an indication of the inadequacy of measures taken to prevent attacks on friendly submarines by the Royal Navy and US Navy but reflects the fact that Britain and America were the only powers engaging in large-scale, offensive, airborne anti-submarine operations in waters used by their own submarines. (Axis airborne ASW was limited to their own littoral waters.) Mistakes were bound to happen. The Western Approaches and Bay of Biscay were highly dangerous areas since they were heavily patrolled by the RAF, hunting U-boats going to and from their bases on the French coast. At the same time British submarines used the area while proceeding to and from the Mediterranean or the Far East. Commander Arthur Pitt of HMS *Taku*:

94

Coming back to the UK from the Mediterranean was a nightmare. Although we were protected by a moving haven I was never confident about the ability of our own aircraft to respect it. The people who really frightened me were those bloody Poles. Even if you painted the boat red, white and blue they would still shoot first and challenge later. Submarine sanctuaries were a contradiction in terms to them.[3]

On 3 September, 1939, the day war was declared, HMS *Sturgeon* (Lieutenant G. D. A. Gregory RN) was bombed while returning to base but sustained no damage. The next day, 4 September, HMS *Seahorse* (Lt D. S. Massy-Dawson RN) was bombed by an RAF aircraft. *Seahorse* dived in a hurry but the after planes jammed and she had to blow main ballast tanks which brought her back to the surface to receive more bombs. She dived again, out of control, and hit the bottom at 240 feet, damaging her Asdic dome. A pyrrhic revenge was extracted on the aircraft, which had been damaged by splinters from one of its own bombs and later had to make a forced landing in the sea. Not all aircraft vs submarine incidents ended thus. A subsequent investigation revealed that the aircraft was considerably off-track. Nevertheless, the route used by submarines entering or leaving Dundee was moved further south and submarine arrival/departure times adjusted to take place at night. Rear Admiral Watson, the head of the Royal Navy's submarine service, ordered that:

> The attention of all Commanding Officers has been drawn to the necessity for firing recognition signals when encountering aircraft thought to be friendly.[4]

The British submarine *L. 27* was attacked in the North Sea while returning from Bergen shortly after this incident. On 5 July, 1940, HMS *Tetrarch* (Lt Cdr R. Mills RN)was attacked by a number of torpedo-armed Swordfish aircraft off the Norwegian coast. The Swordfish was returning from an unsuccessful attempt to find a German cruiser and destroyers reported off Bergen when they attacked a target of opportunity, a surfaced submarine, HMS

*Tetrarch,* some forty miles off the Norwegian coast. The aircraft claimed a success since an explosion was observed and the submarine observed to sink. The explosion was most likely a result of two torpedoes colliding. *Tetrarch* was undamaged but reported a loud explosion when she had reached 90 feet.

The attack took place in a Total Bombing Restriction Area. However, Vice Admiral Commanding Orkneys and Shetlands, Vice Admiral Sir Hugh Binney, who ordered the air strike, commented that he was not aware of the restriction. The leader of the Swordfish squadron had not been informed either, on the grounds that the aircraft had insufficient endurance to affect British submarine operations. Moreover, it was not thought necessary to warn aircraft armed with torpedoes and sent to attack a cruiser about the movements of a friendly submarine. *Tetrarch* made no attempt to identify herself to the aircraft, but was considered to have acted correctly since she was in a restriction area. Three weeks earlier *U-99* (*Kapitän-Leutnant* Otto Kretschmer) had been forced to dive suddenly when attacked by an Ar-196 aircraft from the battle-cruiser *Scharnhorst.* Kretschmer made no attempt to identify himself but dived quickly into safety. No casualties were suffered in the attack but light damage was sustained, though not sufficient to warrant the submarine coming off patrol.

Almost a year after her first experience at the hands of the Fleet Air Arm, HMS *Tetrarch* was attacked by an RAF Blenheim on 28 August, 1941, while the submarine was on patrol in the Gulf of Sirte. The aircraft strafed the submarine with machine-gun fire and then dropped four 250lb bombs which fortunately all failed to explode. *Tetrarch* was in a restriction area and the pilot was aware of this. However, when the submarine failed to identify herself, the pilot assumed she was hostile and attacked. The reason no identification had been offered was that neither the OOW nor the lookouts had seen the aircraft and the first indication they had was when the aircraft attacked with machine-gun fire!

In the Pacific the American submarines had their own problems with friendly aircraft. USS *Thresher's* ordeal on 7 and 8 December, 1941, has already been referred to but there were many others. On 20 December, 1941, USS *Pompano* was attacked twice by friendly aircraft while en route to her patrol area off the Solomon Islands.

In February, 1942, USS *Gudgeon* was attacked by carrierborne aircraft near Marcus Island. On 4 March, 1942, USS *Sargo* was attacked by an RAAF aircraft while on passage to Fremantle and on 7 June, 1942, USS *Grayling* was mistaken for the damaged Japanese cruiser *Mogami* following the Battle of Midway. She was attacked and claimed as sunk, a claim hotly disputed when the submarine returned to harbour. No casualties or serious damage was sustained in these attacks, but the Americans began to establish the most elaborate measures to ensure the separation of friendly submarines and aircraft.

One of the strangest such stories concerns the French submarine *Surcouf*. *Surcouf* was a large cruiser submarine built in 1929 with a displacement of 3250 tons. She was designed for commerce warfare, the *guerre de corse* which had long been a central element of French naval strategy, and was armed with two 8-inch guns in addition to her more conventional armament of eight 21-inch and four 15. 7-inch torpedo tubes. For long-range reconnaissance she carried a Besson MB411 floatplane in a watertight hangar on the casing. When the Germans invaded France in 1940 *Surcouf* was in refit at Brest but managed to escape to Devonport. There she was taken over by the Royal Navy in Operation *Catapult* in July, 1940: two British personnel were killed while doing so. The British, faced with the problem of what to do with this monster submarine, felt that she should be moored somewhere out of the way and forgotten about. Her machinery and armament were incompatible with British equipment and there was no hope of getting spares from France. De Gaulle would have none of it. *Surcouf,* the largest submarine in the world, was a symbol of French greatness.

So began a miserable saga in which the British tried to keep the submarine operational while her crew, drafted from such French naval personnel who opted to join the Free French cause, grew steadily more disenchanted. Rumours about her loyalty or otherwise multiplied.[5] In the end Vice Admiral Horton decided to send her off to the Pacific to guard French possessions in Polynesia, thereby killing two birds with one stone: satisfying the French that *Surcouf* was still useful and getting rid of her to another theatre of operations.

Accordingly *Surcouf* was sailed from Halifax, Nova Scotia, via

Bermuda and the Panama Canal to Tahiti and New Caledonia. Up to now it has always been suggested that she was sunk in collision with the American freighter *Thompson Lykes* on 18 February, 1942. There were no survivors. However, attention has focused on the circumstances of the sinking and there is room for believing that *Surcouf* was not the victim of the collision. The evidence for this centres around the positions for the two ships at the time collision occurred. *Surcouf*'s estimated position and that of the *Thompson Lykes* are about fifty miles apart, though this can easily be explained away as navigational error. However, further doubt has been cast on the collision theory as a result of analysis of photographs of damage to the bows of the *Thompson Lykes* taken after the collision. The energy expended by a mass of 6,000 tons (*Thompson Lykes'* displacement) striking another while moving at 13 knots, which was her speed at the time of the collision, is more than sufficient to cause major structural damage which would have required major repairs. The photographs show no such damage.[6] If *Thompson Lykes* did not strike *Surcouf*, then what did she collide with? Several members of her crew described the object as a launch of some description but this has always been discounted in view of the fact that if a launch or small tanker had been lost then her failure to return to port would have been noticed. However, the ship struck by the *Lykes* might have been a smuggler's launch, whose absence would not have been reported.

A few days after the collision reports were heard of an attack on a submarine by two A-17 aircraft and a B-18 from the US Army Air Force's 3rd Bombardment Squadron flying from Rio Hata in the Panama Canal Zone. The orders to attack a submarine were received from 6th Bombardment Group HQ in Panama at 0713 on 19 February. The attack took place in an area where *Surcouf* would have been had she continued along her course to Colon, the eastern end of the Panama Canal. She was travelling in a moving haven but there is no record of the 3rd Bombardment Squadron aircrew being briefed about this before they took off, although all US commands in the area had been issued with details of her route. Lieutenant Harold Staley was the pilot of one of the A-17's and recalled that the submarine, "a very large one", was lying very low in the water and, after Staley had dropped four 100lb bombs, she drifted towards the coast and sank off the island of Chi Chi Mey in the Archipelago de las Mulatas. Bodies were washed ashore and buried by local Indians near San Blas Point. Unfortunately, although the details of the attack are recorded in the operational records of the 3rd Bombardment Squadron, there are no records of the operational orders from 6th Bombardment Group, or of how they learned of the submarine's presence. The end of the *Surcouf* is shrouded in mystery, but there is considerable doubt over whether she was sunk by collision. On the other hand there is insufficient evidence to say categorically that she was the victim of friendly fire. As she did in life, *Surcouf* continues to perplex and confuse the historian.

Back in home waters, on 28 April, 1942, HMS *Sturgeon* was part of the escort for convoy PQ. 15 heading for Russia when she was attacked by a Northrop floatplane from 330 (Norwegian) Squadron based in Iceland. The aircraft "apologized" to HMS *Ledbury*, one of the convoy's destroyer escorts, and the senior RAF officer in Iceland commented that he had not warned the Northrop about the convoy, or that the convoy would have two submarines as part of the escort, on the grounds that he thought that the aircraft would not fly sufficiently far to sight the convoy and so, on security grounds, there was no need for the aircrew to know about the convoy. The known activities of German agents in Iceland may have been a factor in keeping knowledge of the convoy's movements tightly restricted.

One of the few such incidents involving the *Kriegsmarine* also took place in the Arctic. In the mêlée following the scattering of convoy PQ. 17 in July, 1942, U-boats and the *Luftwaffe* were left to mop up the straggling merchant ships which were all trying to make for Archangel individually or in small groups. The tactical situation was extremely confused and after *U-334* (*Kapitän-Leutnant* Wilmar Simeon) had sunk the freighter *Earlston* on 5 July his submarine was bombed by a marauding Ju. 88. Sufficient damage was caused to make Simeon break off his patrol and he had to be escorted back to Kirkenes by *U-456*.

Undoubtedly the submarine to suffer the most damage as a result of an attack by a friendly aircraft was HMS *Thrasher*. *Thrasher* sailed from Port Said for patrol on the evening of 26 July, 1942.

Her Commanding Officer, Lieutenant Commander Hugh Mackenzie RN (now Vice-Admiral Sir Hugh Mackenzie) later recalled that they were:

> proceeding on the surface, zig-zagging with a safety corridor around us to prevent attack by friendly aircraft. At about 9pm I came down from the bridge to have supper thinking that everything was all settled; we were about thirty miles outside Port Said then, happily on our way. I was sitting at my usual place at the wardroom table, which was in the gangway as near to the control room as possible, so that I could get out in a hurry if needed, and I remember very clearly something telling me to get out on the bridge and I got up and left the table without explaining why, or in response to any request for me to go on the bridge. I was just going through the watertight bulkhead between the wardroom and the control room when there was the most God-awful explosion and the next thing I remember was picking myself up from the after end of the control room up against the W/T office. During the course of getting up from there I remember seeing the ship's galley range which was in the passageway abaft the wireless office leave the ship's side in a cloud of blue sparks.
>
> As I was picking myself up I heard the OOW, the first lieutenant, giving the order to dive and the drill was carried out. The vents were opened by the outside ERA although the lights had gone out and there were a lot of odd noises going on. I then heard the Bren gun on the bridge open fire so I knew they were all right up there. The signalman, lookouts and OOW came down and we dived. Reports were coming in of damage: quite clearly we had no electrical power, smoke was coming from the battery compartments, we had a fire in the battery (smoke and gas were coming from Nos 2 & 3 and No 1 battery was on fire and later had to be flooded with distilled water) and we had to drop all the main fuses, but we sorted ourselves out. The gyro was humming like an

angry bee and the magnetic compass was upside down and no good. It seemed to me that the best thing we could do would be to get back on the surface, especially as the first lieutenant thought it was a Swordfish which had attacked us.

It was indeed a Swordfish which was responsible for the attack which had been carried out at 2140 in position 31°N 32°E, in the middle of a submarine "sanctuary" where a total bombing restriction was in force. The Swordfish, from 815 Squadron (a Fleet Air Arm Squadron) and flown by Sub-Lieutenant D. Stuart RNVR, was on anti-submarine patrol and was armed with four 250lb depth charges. The aircrew were not advised of the sanctuary when they took off from El Gamil airfield and all attempts to contact the plane after she had taken off were unsuccessful. It should be remembered that the Navy was still smarting over the loss of the submarine depot ship HMS *Medway*[7] at the end of June and that Rear Admiral Philip Vian had ordered a maximum effort in anti-submarine operations as a result. Ken Sunor was a Telegraphist Air Gunner (TAG) with 815 Squadron and at the time was waiting at the airfield to take off on the next patrol. He recalled that:

I was due to take off on the next patrol so was sat in the W/T van when our duty officer arrived – in some concern. Could the Tel raise the aircraft in the air and send an NYKO message? It warned him of the *Thrasher* – information only just received. But as we called, so the aircraft sent us his message that he had attacked. It was too late.[8]

The Swordfish dropped all four charges: one fell on the port side abreast the fore hatch and exploded under the ship, two others fell on the starboard side abreast the after end of the midships external torpedo tubes while the last was not seen to explode. The force of the three explosions lifted the stern so much that *Thrasher*'s bows were driven under water. Now Mackenzie had to bring his crippled boat back to harbour:

101

It was quite clear that we could not proceed with the patrol so we surfaced and then had to try to get our engines started with no electrical power which took a little time. . . . We got the engines going but our main problem was to keep afloat because the main ballast tanks were leaking the whole time and we had to keep blowing them with high-pressure air since there was no electric power to use the LP blower. We'd got no means of steering a proper course since all the compasses were gone. Fortunately it was a starlit night and I knew that Port Said was roughly south so I directed operations standing on the bridge with the Pole Star behind me saying "Port" and "Starboard" down the voicepipe. We then ran into one of the trawlers patrolling off Port Said and identified ourselves. We staggered into Port Said on our last gasp of high-pressure air . . . our ballast tanks were awash.[9]

Captain (S)1, Captain S. M. Raw RN, commented that *Thrasher's* "excellent construction was very severely tested and proved thoroughly sound".[10] The list of damage to *Thrasher* covered two sides of densely typed foolscap and, in the totality of the damage sustained in this attack, *Thrasher* has the dubious claim to being the most damaged British submarine of the war. The most serious damage was to the battery where only thirty of the 336 cells were undamaged. The list covers forty-two other defects ranging from a weakness in the pressure hull between frames 87 and 88 where the plates were working slightly to the fact that every porcelain lavatory bowl and basin on board was smashed. Despite this extensive list of damage Captain Raw felt moved to write to the Admiralty that:

The 250lb depth charge is not big enough. Many have felt this for some time.[11]

The RAF, under whose control the Swordfish was operating, launched an enquiry into the incident under the auspices of 201 Group. Ken Sunor recalled that:

There was of course an enquiry. The aircrew said that it (the submarine) was outside the sanctuary. The *Thrasher* of course said they were inside. At that distance from the coast and with radar I don't think the aircrew were much in error – it was probably a borderline case – but a more mature crew might have given the submarine the benefit of the doubt. But remember the prior attitude of Admiral Vian, "Get that submarine at all costs!" Now he wanted to know, "Can't you recognize a T-boat when you see one!"[12]

Sadly no trace of the proceedings of the enquiry into the *Thrasher* incident can be found. Shortly after *Thrasher*'s ordeal, HMS *Talisman* (Lieutenant-Commander M. Willmott RN), a T class submarine of the same class but of an earlier group, was attacked by a Sunderland flying boat. The submarine was proceeding on a northerly course at 13. 5 knots on the surface when shortly after 1400 a Sunderland was sighted on a southerly course about six miles away. Willmott assumed that the aircraft had not seen his submarine and decided that the safest thing to do was to dive quietly out of sight without making a recognition signal. Weather conditions were excellent with a clear sky and superb visibility.

Accordingly *Talisman* dived to 45 feet then came back up to periscope depth to check if the aircraft had passed. At this stage the trim (the fore and aft balance of a submarine when dived) was lost and *Talisman* broke surface in full view of the Sunderland which had seen the submarine and which was now attacking. Willmott ordered the quick diving tanks, "Q" tanks holding ten tons of water, flooded to increase depth:

> when at 47 feet and about 4 degrees bow down a pattern of depth charges straddled the submarine's stern, three on the port side and one on the starboard side. The third and fourth depth charges were the heaviest (the aircraft attacked from west to east and all depth charges seemed to explode within three seconds of each other) and the after planes and steering gear were put out of action.[13]

The bow-down angle increased to 10° and the explosions forced *Talisman* down to a depth of 355 feet – well below her designed depth of 300 feet. Drastic action was required to halt the dive, yet Willmott could not risk disclosing the boat's position through too violent blowing of the ballast tanks for fear of a further attack. Instead he managed to arrest the initial deep dive at 200 feet and then allowed the boat to increase depth gradually while at the same time altering course.

In his comments on the incident Flag Officer Submarines, Vice Admiral Max Horton, noted that *Talisman* was not fully worked up, having just come out of refit and having had a change in personnel. Horton gave credit to Willmott whose:

> experience and cool handling saved what might have been a disaster, though he was himself to blame for the incident which might have caused this disaster.[14]

In retrospect Willmott would have done better to have identified himself to the aircraft before diving, given the good visibility and that he was not in a submarine sanctuary. However, his caution, in view of the number of attacks on submarines by "friendly" aircraft, is understandable. The Sunderland's crew had acted quite correctly in attacking a submarine which made no attempt to identify herself and which dived shortly after being sighted. A month after this incident *Talisman* was lost with all her crew: she is believed to have been mined off Sicily on or around 17 September, 1942.

The list continues: on 19 August, 1942, HMS *Seraph* was attacked in the Atlantic by a RAF Whitley; on 21 August, 1942, HMS *Taku* was attacked off Beirut by an RAF Wellington and on 26 October, 1942, HMS *Sealion* was attacked by an RAF Whitley in the Bay of Biscay. In each case the submarine was in a Total Bombing Restriction Area. The attack on *Taku* illustrated the dilemma faced by a submarine when friendly aircraft were sighted. The standing instructions for British submarines were to dive while firing a recognition signal. The disadvantage here lay in the fact that the aircraft was likely to view the submarine diving as an "admission of guilt" and act accordingly. Alternatively the submarine was to remain on the surface but not fire a recognition signal and trust that the aircraft would observe any restrictions in force. Under these circumstance the submarine could, at the discretion of the Commanding Officer, issue the signal letter challenge. Submarines were in an invidious position.

On this occasion *Taku*'s standing orders were that, if sighted at night by friendly aircraft, the submarine should not indicate her presence. It was only after two depth charges had fallen alongside the submarine that a flare was fired together with a three-star recognition grenade. Captain (S) One, Captain Philip Ruck-Keene considered that he found:

> the bombing of the submarine in the sanctuary when all authorities had been informed of her presence quite unintelligible. The pilot had ample time and light to recognize not only the appearance and silhouette but also the complete dissimilarity to any Axis U-boat. In any case what U-boat would remain passively on the surface for that period of time. *(The Wellington had observed Taku for 45 minutes before making the attack – author.)*[15]

Nevertheless Ruck-Keene felt that *Taku* should have identified herself. However, when the papers reached the Admiralty, they considered that *Taku* had acted quite correctly. A subsequent enquiry by 201 Group RAF found that the aircraft was 60 miles out of position. The navigator responsible was posted away from the Squadron for further training.

On 11 November, 1942, the first submarine was sunk in an encounter with an aircraft of her own side. Under the command of Lieutenant Commander E. A. Woodward HMS *Unbeaten* was one of the most successful submarines in the famous 10th Submarine Flotilla operating from Malta. In the autumn of 1942 *Unbeaten* returned to the UK for a routine refit before sailing, now under the command of Lieutenant Donald Watson, for a patrol in the Bay of Biscay on 23 October, 1942. She was ordered to intercept an outward-bound blockade runner and on 6 November reported the ship but did not attack. Nothing was ever heard from the submarine again.

When *Unbeaten* failed to make her rendezvous off the Bishop's Rock an investigation into her likely fate was begun. In the course of the investigation it was found that an attack on a submarine in *Unbeaten*'s area had been made by Wellington F Freddie of 172 Squadron. The aircraft had taken off at 1745 on 10 November and the patrol report states that:

> At 0300 in position 46° 55'N, 08°43' W a message from base was received diverting "F" to attack a submarine reported in position 46°13'N, 07°40'W at 2120 and steering 040° true. Speed 15 knots. At 0129 in position 48°00'N 07°44'W aircraft set course for estimated position of the submarine. At 0216 a S/E contact was obtained 8 miles 20° to port. Aircraft then homed to within three miles when severe S/E interference was encountered. A course of 180° true was held and at 3/4 mile range a submarine was sighted by L/E dead ahead.
>
> The submarine was fully surfaced and on a course of 347° true. speed 12-15 knots. "F" was flying at 200' and at 0222 in position 46° 50'N, 06° 51'W made a steep dive down to starboard down to 75' in an endeavour to drop the depth charges ahead of the submarine . . . A column of water was observed to envelop the stern of the submarine and it was estimated that at least two explosions straddled the submarine which made a 90° turn to port and remained stationary at right-angles to its original course. Aircraft then made three further runs on the target.[16]

This attack was within the bombing restriction area and in a position within 10 miles of *Unbeaten*'s estimated position. An investigation of the relevant German and Italian records show that it was not one of their boats which was the victim of the attack, nor do the Axis claim to have sunk an Allied submarine in the area at the time. Despite this evidence and other circumstantial evidence, such as the fact that the S/E interference experienced by "F" Freddie was probably caused by *Unbeaten*'s Type 291 air warning set, an RAF Board of Enquiry failed to come to any conclusions.

Officially the file on the loss of HMS *Unbeaten* remains open, but it is almost certain that "F" Freddie was responsible for her loss.

The list continues: two of the boats of the US Navy's Submarine Squadron 50 (SubRon50), USS *Gunnel* and *Shad*, which had been deployed to the North Atlantic in support of the Royal Navy during Operation *Torch*, were attacked by British aircraft owing to faulty recognition procedures; on 21 January, 1943, HMS *Safari* was attacked north east of Algiers; on 7 February the USS *Swordfish* had to return from patrol early after being attacked and badly damaged by a USAAC B-17 north of New Zealand (permanent repairs were subsequently undertaken at Mare Island); in April, 1943, USS *Harder* was attacked by a US Navy PBM-3 Mariner while on passage between New London and the Panama Canal and on 7 June, 1943, HMS *Sceptre* was attacked by an RAF Hampden in a designated exercise area (in this case the aircraft made the correct recognition signal after the attack).

# CHAPTER EIGHT

## *Aircraft vs Submarines (ii)*

It looks as though the pilots who carried out the attack should be
told that their shooting was good.

*Lieutenant J. M. Maas Royal Netherlands Navy after being strafed by
RAF Mosquitoes, January 1945.*

The "Fog of War" is a phrase that easily, sometimes too easily,
springs to mind when describing, or accounting for, these incidents. However, the sinking of the Italian submarine *Topazio* on 12
September, 1943, is a case where the "Fog" was particularly im-
penetrable. Under the terms of the armistice concluded with the
Allies by the Italian government led by Marshal Pietro Badoglio
the Italians were required to send a large portion of their fleet,
including all submarines, into internment at Malta or some other
designated port.

On 12 September *Topazio* was proceeding on the surface south-
east of Cape Carbonara on the south-east coast of Sardinia when she
was attacked and sunk by an RAF aircraft. The attack was particularly unfortunate since it took place in an area where a "real"
U-boat had been sighted only fourteen hours earlier and that
*Topazio* was one of the *Sirena* class submarines which had had their
bulky conning towers cut down so that they bore an uncanny
resemblance to the ubiquitous German Type VII U-boat. A further
complicating factor was that the submarine was not displaying the
standard recognition symbols which had been ordered for surren-
dering Italian forces, precisely to prevent this sort of incident.

A number of *Topazio*'s crew survived the attack but none was saved. Although ships and aircraft proceeded to the scene of the attack for rescue duties, the search was abandoned when the staff at Malta decided that the submarine in question was the Italian *Turkese* which had since been sighted en route for North Africa and internment. It may be argued that this incident should not be listed as friendly fire, but the incident does illustrate the importance of displaying correct and readily identifiable identification signals. In the confusion which attended the Italian surrender in an active theatre of war, the *Topazio* was a victim of circumstances for which the agents of her loss were in no way to blame.

In the early hours of 13 September, 1943, HMS *Sportsman* (Lt R. G. Gatehouse RN) was operating south-west of the Bonifacio Strait in the Mediterranean in a Total Bombing Restriction area when she was attacked by a Liberator:

> 0351/13. Straddled by four depth charges. The OOW (Lieutenant A. H. Anderson RNR) saw this plane about half a mile away approaching at 40' from down moon. Position 40° 29'N, 06° 40'E (DR). It was a four-engined machine. These facts are corroborated by the Engineer Officer who was on the bridge at the time. Lieutenant Anderson ordered the lookouts below and immediately after this saw four depth charges leave the machine. One burst shallow and severely burnt him with flash. Down below I got the impression that the whole boat lifted, while the engine room say the engines took off. I arrived on the bridge to find Lieutenant Anderson in a state of collapse but he managed to get below unassisted. No sooner had I asked for a report on damage than I heard the machine and realized diving must be accepted.
>
> 0351/15. Dived. Most electrical auxiliary machinery was off the board, plane indicators, steering motor, order instruments etc and I regret to say that we came up to 20 again. When passing through 40' on our way down again, we got one more charge which put many lights out and flooded the conning tower. We retired to 80' to put ourselves in order and curse the RAF.

0532. surfaced. The bridge was severely damaged. My recollections are that after the first pattern, the only damage was that our defective radar aerial had been blown over the side. Now the brass coaming of the conning tower had been blown between the upper lid and its seat and had parted the port clip fastening studs. The port after bridge plating was severely damaged, the radar was heavily bent, telegraphs blown off the after standard and all electrical apparatus smashed. When the conning tower was pumped out , a portion of a British Mk X depth charge pistol was found in the bottom and the case of the depth charge was on the Oerlikon platform.[1]

The Liberator was from the 480th A/S Group USAAC and according to Captain (S) Eight were "strange to Mediterranean conditions". The aircrew were interviewed and stated that they dropped a pattern of seven torpex filled 350lb depth charges, spaced 60' apart and set to explode at 25'. One fell some distance away but one of the others was observed to give off such a blinding flash on exploding that the aircrew thought that the attack must have been successful. As a result they did not pursue their second bombing run with their remaining three charges. One of the depth charges hit the Type 291 radar aerial, knocking out the pistol. The torpex then spilled out and ignited which was what caused the horrific burns to Lieutenant Anderson (who was a "spare" submarine Commanding Officer embarked in *Sportsman* for "experience"). It was the pistol from this charge which was found in the conning tower and the case on the Oerlikon platform.

In view of the fact that the Liberator only carried out one attack, the second explosion which rocked the boat so badly, and which accounted for most of the damage, must have come from a second depth charge which lodged on the bridge and which did not explode until *Sportsman* reached 25'. It was incredible that no serious structural damage to the hull was sustained, although the explosive power of the depth charge would have undoubtedly been lessened on account of it being damaged when it struck the bridge. In what was a rare occurrence, the Air Officer Commanding North

110

West African Coastal Air Force and his deputy personally visited *Sportsman* to convey their apologies for the incident. *Sportsman's* survival was a testament to the rugged construction of British submarines and also the sound practice of having both an upper and a lower hatch to the conning tower. Nine days later the Polish submarine *Dzik* in (commanded by Lt Cdr B. S. Romanowski whom we last met while in command of the unfortunate *Jastrazb*) was bombed by the USAAC off Algiers. Fortunately no damage or casualties were sustained. On 10 October, 1943, the French submarine *Minerve* was attacked and damaged by an aircraft of RAF Coastal Command off the Scilly Islands. The aircraft attacked with rockets which killed two of her crew and partially disabled her. No further information is available on this incident.

Only two American submarines were lost in the Atlantic during the Second World War. The old *S-26* was rammed accidentally by *PC-460* on 24 January, 1942, in a marine accident. However, the loss of the submarine *Dorado* in October, 1943, is attributable to a number of reasons, including an attack by American aircraft. USS *Dorado* under the command of Lieutenant Commander Earle C. Schneider was a brand new *Gato* class submarine which left the submarine base at New London, Connecticut, on 6 October, 1943, en route for the Pacific via the Panama Canal. She was never heard from again. At 2051 on 13 October in the Caribbean (15°, 21'N, 73°, 13'W) a PBM-3 aircraft of the US Navy carried out a depth-charge attack on a submarine. The aircraft under the command of Lieutenant (jg) D. T. Felix USN, detected the submarine on the surface at 2030 hours. At 2030 *Dorado* was reported as being in position 15 30'N, 72°, 40'W about forty eight miles away bearing 100° and steering a course of 243 (true). The submarine sighted by the aircraft was steering 310° on an intercept course with convoy GAT92. The submarine was clearly seen by the aircraft crew who identified her as having the characteristics of a minelayer. At 2051 the aircraft dropped three Mk. 47 depth charges and one Mk. 4 Mod 4 demolition bomb. One depth charge and the bomb failed to explode and no explosion was seen from the other two depth charges. The aircraft made a second pass over the area using flares to illuminate the scene but saw nothing other than bubbles and white water.

111

A second contact was made at 2240 and, after attempts to exchange recognition signals failed, the submarine fired on the aircraft while taking evasive action. Momentarily the plane and submarine were hidden from each other by a rain squall and by the time the plane emerged the submarine had gone. Further searches by aircraft and *PC-1251* failed to find the submarine, although some debris of indeterminate origin was found.

When *Dorado* failed to arrive at Colon her movements were analysed against aircraft operations and it appeared that she would have been in the area where the PBM-3 carried out the attack. However, after the war, when it became possible to study the German U-boat records, it appears that this explanation for *Dorado's* loss may be too simple. In the area at the same time was the German *U-214* (*Kapitän-Leutnant* Rupprecht Stock). Stock had been busy laying a field of fifteen mines off the entrance to the Panama Canal on 8 October. He then laid two EMS mines east of the Antilles between 13 and 14 October. On 13 October Stock reported that he too was attacked by an aircraft, although his patrol report only mentions one attack. However, if the depth charges and the demolition bomb dropped by the PBM in the first attack failed to explode, it is quite possible that Stock was not even aware that he was under attack. Stock's report then mentions sighting flares which could well have been the aircraft and PC-1251 searching. Either Dorado or U-214 could have been the victims of the air attack.

If it was not *Dorado,* what other explanations exist for her loss? U-214's mines are the most likely reason. *Dorado* would have been in the vicinity of the first field almost immediately after they had been laid. The mines were not detected until 16 October and then only ten were recovered. The remainder were never swept. Of the other two mines laid off the Antilles, U-214 heard a loud explosion followed by other noises coming from the area of the lay between 1648 and 1707 on 15 October. This could well have been *Dorado* as she would have been in the area at the time and no other vessels were reported lost in that area at the time. Who knows? The case of USS *Dorado* remains open.

July, 1944, saw the loss of two submarines at the hands of friendly aircraft. The French *La Perle* was a mine-laying submarine of the *Saphir* class built at Toulon and launched on 30 July, 1935. In addition to her armament of three 550mm torpedo tubes and two 400mm triple torpedo mountings, she carried 32 mines in external wells housed in the ballast tanks. *La Perle* avoided decommissioning under the terms of the 1940 Armistice with Germany and at the end of 1942 was on a routine transit to Dakar when the Anglo-American forces invaded North Africa and she came over to the Allied side. In 1943 and early 1944 she participated in a number of special operations in the Mediterranean and Bay of Biscay before proceeding to the USA for a much-needed refit.

On 8 July, 1944, *La Perle* was returning to the Mediterranean after a refit in Philadelphia Navy Yard when she was bombed and sunk by Swordfish aircraft operating from the MAC ships[2] *Empire Maccoll* and *Empire Maccallum* which were part of the escort for convoy ONM. 243. There was one survivor, Chief Petty Officer Emile Cloarec, who was picked up by HMCS *Hespeler*. He reported that fifteen of *La Perle*'s ship's company of fifty-eight officers and men had escaped from the submarine before she sank but the others had been unable to keep afloat.

That the attack should have occurred at all was a cause for concern. *La Perle*, under the command of *Capitaine de Corvette* Tachin, left New London, Connecticut, on 26 June for St John's, Newfoundland, under escort by the American destroyer *Cockerel*. After a short stay in Newfoundland she sailed for Holy Loch in the UK. In coastal waters she was escorted by the Canadian destroyer *Chicoutimi* but would make the crossing of the Atlantic alone and travelling on the surface.

Sailing across the Atlantic at the same time and on a roughly similar course was the Halifax-Clyde convoy ONM. 243 which included the MAC ships *Empire Maccoll* and *Empire Maccallum*. The convoy was escorted by the C. 5 escort group commanded by Acting Commander C. H. Stephen OBE, DSC, RCNR, in the destroyer HMCS *Dunver*. The Escort Group, since sailing, had received daily situation reports from Western Approaches headquarters at Liverpool which included details of *La Perle*'s movements. However, signals advising 'friendly' forces of the bombing restrictions in force around *La Perle*'s likely position were not passed to the Escort Group. But adequate information was

113

available to Commander Stephen to indicate that *La Perle* would pass sufficiently close to the convoy to be within the area covered by his air patrols. This was realized by him and he sent two signals on 7 July warning of *La Perle's* proximity to the convoy. The signals were to be passed by HMCS *Dunver* to the convoy commodore, vice-commodore and the MAC ships, but the correct procedure was not carried out and the signals were not received in the MAC ships. As no evidence was available from the commodore's ship it is not possible to establish why the procedure was not adhered to.

Prior to the convoy sailing a general agreement with regard to air patrols was made by telephone between Commander Stephen and the Air Staff Officer in *Empire Maccoll*, Lieutenant Commander Neale. No patrol orders were given to the MAC ships while at sea, so no special precautions were taken to advise aircrew prior to morning patrols on 8 July that a friendly submarine was in the area. Stephen may also have been lulled into a false sense of security by a message, received at 0038Z on 8 July from Western Approaches headquarters, which placed the submarine, wrongly, further away from the convoy than she actually was.

*La Perle* was first sighted by a Swordfish at 1253Z. The pilot, Lieutenant Otterveanger, an officer of the Royal Netherlands Navy, resolved to shadow the submarine and call up reinforcements rather than make an immediate attack which he felt might not be successful given the quick diving time of a U-boat. He noticed the recognition signals made by *La Perle* but disregarded them. Between the time of *La Perle* being sighted and the attack being carried out an interval of more than an hour elapsed. Surprisingly neither the pilot nor the air staff in *Empire Maccoll* thought it strange that the supposed "U-boat" should remain on the surface keeping a steady course and doing an estimated fifteen knots while making no attempt to dive into safety. It was not until 1358Z that Stephen realized that the submarine which his aircraft were bent on destroying might be *La Perle*. Even then there was no degree of urgency about his signal and no attempt was made to halt the attack by communicating directly with the aircraft. Stephen's failure to realize the situation was probably due to the latest Admiralty Intelligence report indicating that a U-boat might be in the vicinity of the convoy.

Before take-off the aircraft were advised of the current recognition signals then in force. On sighting the aircraft *La Perle* made the correct signals in good faith, having been informed of the total bombing and attack restrictions in force around her, which were totally disregarded by the aircraft. Presumably because the pilots had not been warned of *La Perle*'s presence, they disregarded any signals coming from a potentially hostile submarine. Once Otterveanger had been joined by the other seven Swordfish, he led the attack, dropping three depth charges alongside the submarine. The explosions stove in *La Perle*'s hull in the region of the control room causing flooding which in turn caused electrical fires. Chief Petty Officer Emile Cloarec had just asked permission to spend a quarter of an hour on the bridge when the attack began. In French submarines directly beneath the bridge was a small compartment containing the attack instruments and known as the "*kiosque*". It was in this compartment that Cloarec was standing since the bridge was occupied by all five of the submarine's officers and a quartermaster. The fire in the control room vented up through the conning tower and most of the men there and the officers on the bridge were horribly burned. Lieutenant Zappert, the Royal Navy liaison officer, fired off a number of Very cartridges indicating that the submarine was "friendly", but to no avail.

On receiving reports from inside the submarine that the fire and flooding were out of control, Commandant Tachin gave the order to abandon ship. *La Perle* began to settle by the stern and sank twelve minutes after the Swordfish attack. Cloarec, together with fourteen other members of the crew, were left swimming. One by one the Frenchmen drowned or succumbed to exposure until only Cloarec was left alive. He was eventually picked up by the Canadian destroyer *Hespeler* which had been detached by Stephen to look for survivors. He was practically unconscious and initially taken for a German seaman. It was only when he was heard to speak French, *Hespeler* having a number of French Canadians in her ship's company, that the awful truth of what had happened was confirmed.[3]

The French Navy received an expression of regret from A. V. Alexander, the First Lord of the Admiralty, for what had happened but it was not enough. The French wanted a full-scale enquiry which was held under chairmanship of Rear Admiral Lionel Murray CBE, Commander in Chief Canadian North West Atlantic, at St John's, Newfoundland. The Board found that *La Perle* was sunk at 1410Z on 8 July, 1944, in position 55°27'N 33°50'W by a concentrated attack by Swordfish aircraft from the *Empire Maccoll* and *Empire Maccallum*. If the French wanted blame to be apportioned then they were to be mistaken. Commander Stephen was exonerated as were the aircrew from the MAC ships. Only the signals officer in HMCS *Dunver*, Lieutenant Benson, was reprimanded. The sad affair of *La Perle* is fraught with questions. Why was she given a route that would take her so close to ONM. 243? Why were Stephen's two signals not received in the MAC ships? Why did the aircrew ignore the correct recognition signal when it was fired by *La Perle*? Most important of all, why did *La Perle* not dive, rather than bother with identification, as soon as the Swordfish was sighted at 1253?

In the summer of 1944 a number of British and American vessels were transferred to the Soviet Union in lieu of the Soviets' share of the surrendered Italian fleet, it being impracticable to bring the ex-Italian ships into Home Waters for the transfer to take place. The "package" included the submarines *Sunfish, Unison, Ursula* and *Unbroken*. Small Royal Navy parties were embarked in the submarines to assist the Soviet crews in operating the machinery. Theirs was not a happy experience. They found the discipline in the Soviet Fleet to be harsh and unbending and Soviet society anything but classless, as they observed the officers appropriate the main accommodation area for conversion to cabins while condemning the crew to a cheerless and cramped existence packed into the fore-ends with the reload torpedoes. They also found that the influence of the political officers was all-pervasive. On one occasion in *V. 1* (ex-HMS *Sunfish*) a British Leading Stoker and a Soviet stoker were rigging a chain purchase to lift a cylinder head in the engine room. The political officer appeared and told the pair that in a Socialist society such tasks were done by hand. Evidently dogma carried more weight than sound engineering practice.

116

Worst of all, vodka was substituted for their beloved "tot".

There were representations to naval authority and threats to desert and let the submarine sail without them but to no avail. Anglo-Soviet co-operation and good relations were at stake, so the full weight of naval discipline was applied to ensure that the ratings stayed at their posts, but only three of the party actually sailed with the submarine.[4] Three of the submarines arrived safely, the fourth, *V. 1,* under the command of Captain 3rd Rank Israel Fisanovitch, failed to arrive at Murmansk when expected. A report was subsequently received from an RAF Liberator that it had attacked and sunk a submarine in the Norwegian Sea on 27 July, 1944.

Rear Admiral Egerton, the SBNO (Senior British Naval Officer) North Russia, considered that the submarine sunk by the Liberator could have been *V. 1.* His initial impression was confirmed when *V. 2* (ex-HMS *Unbroken*) arrived on 3 August. Egerton interviewed Leading Telegraphist C. A. Wilkes, one of the British liaison party on board the submarine, who told him that the Soviet Commanding Officer had not kept to the "safe" route allocated to him and that recognition flares were never kept on the bridge where they were immediately accessible. Egerton concluded:

> It seems more than possible therefore that the submarine attacked on 27 July was in fact *V. 1* who was off her route and who had no recognition signals at immediate notice.[5]

Egerton was correct. *V. 1* had been allotted a "safe haven" in which bombing was restricted during the submarine's journey from Lerwick to the Kola Inlet. The position of the "haven" was adjusted each day to correspond to the submarine's track. It will be remembered that, to allow for navigational errors, a strip 20 miles either side of the "haven" was made a total bombing restriction area by night and submerged bombing restriction area by day. The most likely hypothesis for *V. 1*'s end was that she was way out of position, had no recognition signals to hand when the Liberator was sighted, so dived and was attacked. It is worth noting that the aircraft carrying out the attack was out of position by a factor of 90 miles. As a

117

sequel to this incident the Soviet submarine *SHCH-314* was bombed and sunk in error by Soviet aircraft in the Barents Sea on 21 September, 1944. No further information is available concerning this loss.

The last recorded instance of such an attack in Home Waters took place on 10 January, 1945, when the Dutch submarine *Dolfijn* (Lt Cdr J. Maas RNethN) was attacked by an RAF Mosquito while setting out on her working-up patrol following completion of a refit. While running on the surface at ten knots lookouts sighted a single aircraft to port, followed by four twin-engined aircraft coming in from dead ahead. Although he was in a total bombing restriction area, Maas took no chances and dived. As the submarine passed 25' bursts of cannon fire were heard to hit the bridge. Although there were no casualties, both of *Dolfijn*'s periscopes were out of action and she was forced to return to Lerwick. Repairs took some time and the attack effectively ended the war for *Dolfijn*. Concluding his report on the incident Maass noted that:

> It looks as though the pilots who carried out the attack
> should be told that their shooting was good.[6]

When British and Dutch submarines began to join the US Navy in operations in the south-west Pacific from the end of 1944 onwards, measures to prevent attack by friendly aircraft had to be modified accordingly. In the vicinity of the submarine bases at Fremantle, Exmouth Gulf and Subic Bay, submarine sanctuaries were instituted and local escorts provided for submarines entering or leaving harbour. While proceeding to or from patrol submarines went unescorted on the surface. A daily estimate of their position was distributed in a situation report and Allied aircraft were not normally employed over the passage routes and, for those who were, the areas were declared a Total Bombing Restriction.

The operational waters north of the Malay Barrier were divided into Submarine Zones and Blind Bombing Zones. Allied aircraft were forbidden to attack submarines except in the Blind Bombing Zones from which submarines were excluded. This rather draconian separation was on account of the lack of training in ship/submarine recogntion by the USAAC who provided most of

19. Lieutenant Commander Hugh Mackenzie who commanded HMS *Thresher* when she was attacked by a Fleet Air Arm Swordfish and sustained severe damage.

20. Lieutenant Commander H.C. 'Hairy' Browne who was attacked *five* times by the RAF while serving in submarines.

21. Commander Al Bontier of the USS *Seawolf*. (*US National Archives*).

22. *Kapitän-Leutnant* Helmuth von Tippelskirch, commanding officer of *U-439*. (*UBA 1411/2/4*)

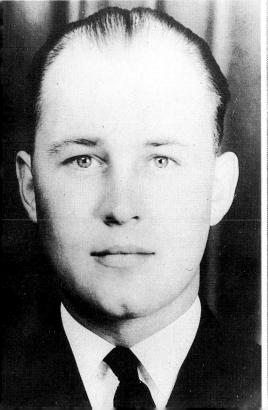

23. Lieutenant Richard Gatehouse (*right*) arriving at Algiers. After being bombed by a B24 Liberator, Gatehouse dived his submarine to 90 feet and "cursed the RAF". In fact his assailant was American.

24. Some of the crew of the British submarine *Talisman*, attacked by a Sunderland and forced down to a depth of 300 feet. (*IWM A.7470*)

25. Lieutenant Commander Boris Romanowski (*centre*) with the crew of the submarine *Dzik*. Romanowski was commanding officer of *P.551* when she was sunk in April, 1942, by HMS *Seagull* and HNorMS *St Albans*, and while in command of *Dzik* was strafed by a Liberator outside Algiers.

26. The combined British and Soviet crews of *Sunfish/V.1* at Rosyth in 1944 after the submarine had been transferred to the USSR. Only three of the British crew sailed with the submarine which was later sunk by an RAF Liberator.

27. The crew of *U-659* sunk in collision with *U-439* on 3 May, 1943, off Cape Finisterre: only three of these men survived. (*UBA 1411/1/1*)

28. The Italian submarine *Topazio* sunk in error by the RAF on 12 September, 1943. Note the German-style conning tower which was a prime factor in her being taken for a U-boat. (*Dott. Achille Rastelli*)

29. *U-439* looking pristine on completion. Only nine were saved from her crew following the collision with *U-659*. (*UBA 1411/2/3*)

30. The French destroyer *Maille Breze* burning at the Tail o' the Bank after one of her own torpedoes exploded onboard in April, 1940.

31. The cruiser HMS *Trinidad* hit by one of her own torpedoes which came back on its track in March, 1942. (*IWM A.8087*)

32. Survivors from *Trinidad* at Greenock on their arrival in the UK in May, 1945. After the ordeal of being hit by one of their own torpedoes, the ship was bombed and sunk while returning to the UK on 15 May, 1942.

33. USS *Tullibee* which was sunk by one of her torpedoes which malfunctioned while attacking a Japanese convoy on 26 March, 1944. (US National Archives).

34. The liner *Arandora Star* in happier days. On 2 July, 1940, she was torpedoed by *U-47* while transporting German PoWs and Italian internees to Canada.

35. Bodies of those killed on the *Cap Arcona* buried in a mass grave at Neustadt in May, 1945, after the ship, containing thousands of concentration camp prisoners, was attacked and sunk by the RAF. (*IWM BU.5457*)

36. *Kapitän-Leutnant* Peter Cremer returning from patrol in happier circumstances than those in which he sank the blockade runner *Spreewald*. (*UBA 1411/1/3*)

37. Commander Richard O'Kane of the USS *Tang* photographed in March, 1946, after his return from Japanese captivity. (*US National Archives*).

the air effort. The policy was therefore to confine bombing operations to areas where they were allowed a free-for-all (the Blind Bombing Zones) and to forbid attacks in other areas even at the risk of passing up some good opportunities. To allow the odd German, Italian or Japanese submarine to escape was considered preferable to sinking one of the many allied boats at sea. The policy had the added advantage from the point of the allied submariners that any aircraft they saw could be assumed to be hostile. Total bombing restrictions were always in force when submarines were employed on air sea rescue ("Lifeguard") operations.[7] Nevertheless the regulations did not always guarantee immunity. USS *Albacore* was attacked twice in three days in November, 1943; *Tunny* was attacked in March, 1944, and *Bullhead* was attacked on 8 April, 1945, while engaged in "Lifeguard" duty. No wonder submariners felt persecuted.

# CHAPTER NINE

## Submarines vs Submarines

The possibility that she was HMS *Swordfish* was not
uppermost in the mind of the Commanding Officer
of HMS *Sturgeon*.

*Captain W. D. Stevens RN commenting on an incident between the two
submarines.*

The greatest efforts were made by naval authorities to keep friendly
submarines apart. Submarines operated on their own and, particularly at night, it was very difficult to distinguish between friend
and foe. The risk of "fratricide", as it was known, was recognized
by the naval staffs of all the belligerents who took careful precautions to prevent it happening. Submarines were assigned
specific areas for their operations in which they were supposed to
remain: navigational problems, however, often resulted in a submarine straying out of her area into another's, often with disastrous
results. The rationale behind these precautions was not only to protect a submarines from the attentions of her own kind, but so that
if another submarine were sighted the Commanding Officer had
complete freedom of action. As Commodore Howard Kelly tren-
chantly reported when commenting on the circumstances
surrounding the loss of the Italian submarine *H-5* on 16 April, 1918,
(torpedoed by the British *H-1* when she strayed out of her area):

> When stationed in definite zones, any submarine sighted
> in that zone must be attacked without hesitation or
> consideration; there can be no question of recognition.[1]

While a submarine was on passage to and from her patrol area, outward and homeward routes would be separated so there was no danger of a chance encounter. If there was chance of two submarines passing while on passage this information would be passed to the boats concerned well in advance. Lastly, considerable importance was given to standard recognition signals by means of the challenge/reply system and colour-coded recognition flares.

These precautions could be double-edged. In 1942 HMS *Upright* was on patrol on the surface in the Mediterranean when, in the early hours of the morning, her lookouts sighted another submarine, also on the surface and on a reciprocal course. In view of the large number of British submarines at sea at the time there was an embargo on attacks on other submarines at night because of the difficulty in identifying another submarine. The two vessels passed at about five cables' distance and when the other submarine was slightly abaft *Upright*'s beam she was identified as a large U-boat. Captain George "Shrimp" Simpson, Commanding Officer of the 10th Submarine Flotilla to which *Upright* belonged, commented that

> another opportunity of destroying the enemy [was] lost through the unfortunate but indispensable necessity of enforcing a submarine "armistice" when more than one submarine is operating in the same area.[2]

It is not recorded whether the U-boat, whose identity is sadly unknown, was operating under a similar embargo, or whether her lookouts simply failed to spot the much smaller British submarine.

Another such example concerned the German U-boat, *U-570*, which had surrendered to the Royal Navy in August, 1941, and which had been put into British service under the name HMS *Graph*. The submarine was generally used for trials purposes but was also sent on a number of operational patrols in the Bay of Biscay where, it was hoped, she could deceive a "genuine" U-boat into allowing her to come close enough to torpedo her. During one such patrol, while on the surface, *Graph* sighted another U-boat, also on the surface. The conditions were perfect for an attack but the "genuine" U-boat's Commanding Officer was taking no chances, for, as soon as he sighted *Graph*, he dived his boat to safety! However, not all submarine v submarine engagements ended in the same way

No sooner had the war begun than the first of these incidents took place. Together with three other submarines HMS *Triton*(Lt Cdr H. P. de C Steele RN) and *Oxley* (Lt Cdr H. G. Bowerman RN) were on reconnaissance patrol off the Norwegian coast. The submarines were disposed in adjoining patrol areas with *Triton* nearest the coast in area 5 and *Oxley* next to her in area 4. At 2004 on the evening of 10 September *Triton* surfaced to begin the daily battery charge. Steele was able to fix her position accurately by taking bearings from the lights at Oberstrad and Kvassheim which placed the submarine slightly to the west and south of her patrol position. Steele resolved to patrol the southern end of his area and set a course 170°. Shortly before 2100 on the evening of 10 September, 1939, *Triton* sighted another submarine on the surface and heading north-west. Steele ordered Leading Signalman Eric Cavanagh to make the challenge by signal lamp. Cavanagh sent the letters "FO" and expected to receive "DY" in return. When no reply was received Steele had it repeated twice before ordering a signal grenade to be fired, which burst correctly. Still no reply, so Steele ordered the attack to begin and fired two torpedoes from *Triton's* external bow tubes. After the torpedoes were fired what was described as an "indeterminate flashing" of a signal lamp was seen coming from the submarine. It was not Morse code, so was disregarded. Then came the explosion of one of *Triton's* torpedoes. Whatever elation *Triton's* ship's company may have felt on achieving their first success so early in the war was quickly dissipated when the two survivors found swimming in the icy water were found to be the Commanding Officer, Lt Cdr H. G. Bowerman, of HMS *Oxley* and a rating, Able Seaman Gluckes.

Why had *Oxley* moved into *Triton's* patrol area and, more importantly, why had she not replied to any of the four challenges? *Oxley* had been occupying the adjoining "billet" to *Triton* and from 1400 onwards on Sunday the 10th she had been at periscope depth proceeding at speeds of between 2 and 3 knots while steering a course of 158°. During the afternoon *Oxley* was communicating regularly with *Triton* by SST and, knowing that *Triton* was in sight of land, Bowerman thought that he was one and half miles within the eastern limit of his sector and eight miles to the south-east of her patrol position and that *Oxley* was bearing 240° and seven miles from *Triton*'s position.

*Oxley* then headed north steering 240° for about two hours before returning to 158°. At 1900 SST contact was re-established with *Triton* and the latter's position was estimated as bearing 010° at a range of 4,900 yards. Bowerman was dubious of this position as it seemed improbable but *Oxley*'s asdic operator was quite definite. However, the contact faded and could not be re-established, so Bowerman concluded that the safest thing to do was to proceed in the direction he was going. In fact *Oxley*'s asdic operator was correct. *Triton* was now very close and *Oxley* was proceeding into her area. Navigation was always difficult for submariners but in this case it was compounded by the very strong tidal sets in the area and Bowerman's reluctance to surface and get an accurate "fix" for fear of being detected by aircraft.

Just after 2030 *Oxley* surfaced for the night. Bowerman could see the lights at Oberstrad and Egero but could not be certain whether it was the actual light he was seeing or merely glare, since there was rain over the land. He thought that he was two miles inside the eastern limit of his sector, whereas in reality he had drifted to a position four miles inside *Triton*'s sector. Bowerman said that after surfacing he had warned the OOW, Lt F. K. Manley RNR, of the possibility of sighting *Triton*, since the two submarines had been in communication by SST[3], and then went below.

A few minutes later Bowerman was called to the bridge:

> On emerging from the upper conning tower hatch the OOW told me that a submarine was just abaft the starboard beam and had fired a grenade. He told me that we had fired a grenade in answer but that it had failed to function. I asked him if we had made the private signal in reply. His answer was "yes" but it must have been hesitant or doubtful because I remember telling him to make it again for certain. He had just commenced making it; I had by this time got out of the conning

123

tower and was looking to starboard to the light. I saw a flash immediately beneath me and heard a dull explosion. The ship seemed to list to port and break in two from the centre.[4]

The subsequent enquiry found that *Oxley* was well to the east of her proper position. The fact that Bowerman could see the lights at Oberstrad and Egero should have warned him of his easterly drift. It would also appear that *Oxley*'s look-outs were not as vigilant as they should have been since *Triton* had had her under observation for some time without being seen in return, and by the time Bowerman was called to the bridge it was too late for him to have any influence on events. The failure of *Oxley*'s grenade was sheer bad luck.

There was never any question of *Triton* being at fault. Indeed Steele was congratulated for his tactical proficiency. Nevertheless the whole affair cast a pall over *Triton*, hitherto a very happy boat. Their Lordships concluded that no blame was attributable to Bowerman either. However, he did not serve in submarines again but reverted to General Service where he was awarded the Distinguished Service Cross and two Mentions in Despatches for service in destroyers. Little was said at the Board of Enquiry about *Oxley*'s OOW, Lieutenant F. K. Manley RNR, although evidence from Bowerman hinted at lax signalling procedures: *de mortuis nil nisi bonum.*

Four days later there was another incident between two British submarines which had more fortunate results than in the case of the *Oxley*. On the night of 13 September, 1939, HMS *Swordfish* (Lieutenant C. B. Crouch RN) was returning to Dundee from patrol. She was travelling at seven knots so as to arrive off the Tay estuary at dawn on the 14th and to reduce the wash over her saddle tanks. At 0043 a darkened vessel was sighted on her port side approaching at speed, roughly 400 yards away. Crouch immediately dived the submarine and put the helm over to starboard. At 0048 a distant explosion was heard and from 0050 Swordfish began transmitting the recognition signal in force using her SST. Two more explosions were heard at 0056 before the submarine surfaced at 0200 and proceeded to Dundee.

It was only later that the identity of the other craft was found to be HMS *Sturgeon* (Lt G. D. A. Gregory RN). *Sturgeon* was leaving Dundee to go on patrol when at 0043 the OOW, Sub Lt M. G. R. Lumby RN (who in time would become a distinguished Commanding Officer in his own right) sighted a submarine passing from starboard to port and crossing *Sturgeon*'s bow at a range of 1500 yards. Gregory's patrol report continues:

> At 0045 the wheel was put to port to bring *Sturgeon* onto a firing course. The three starboard tubes were not ready for firing till 0500, by which time *Sturgeon* and *Swordfish* were on parallel courses. . . . At 0055 *Swordfish* was observed to dive. Starboard wheel was ordered in *Sturgeon* and the tubes were fired at six-second intervals immediately the ship started to swing . . . The tracks were seen to run very distinctly, the first appearing to run over *Swordfish*'s after casing and the remaining two astern.
>
> Throughout the attack there was no doubt in my mind as to the identity of the target. A comparatively small and upright conning tower and the appearance of no periscope standards caused me to classify it as German. The course of 340° confirmed this identification as it was known that no fiendly submarine was proceeding to Aberdeen. Recognition procedure was not carried out.[5]

The subsequent enquiry conducted by Captain W. D. Stephens RN, Captain S2, revealed a highly unsatisfactory state of affairs which:

> is a grave reflection on the inadequacy of the final instructions given to the Commanding Officer of *Sturgeon* before sailing.[6]

No specific instructions had been given to Gregory to the effect that *Swordfish* was on her way back from patrol. It seems that Gregory was expected to find out for himself what friendly forces were in the area by talking to the Flotilla Staff and by reading the

125

"Patrol Boards" in the operations office. Most amazing of all is that the same route was allocated to homeward and outward bound submarines travelling at night – a recipe for disaster if ever there was one. In his report to Rear Admiral B. C. Watson, Rear Admiral (Submarines) and head of the Navy's submarine service, Stephens reported:

> Separate outward and homeward tracks to and from the Tay have now been instituted and in addition a forecast of all relevant movements is being included in the written patrol orders given to each submarine.[7]

However, Watson was not inclined to letter the matter rest. Both Stephens and Gregory were summoned to RA(S)'s wartime headquarters at Aberdour for an interview:

> I have informed Captain(S), 2nd Submarine Flotilla that such a serious mistake in his organization must not be allowed to occur again. I have also seen the Captain of *Sturgeon* and informed him that he acted incorrectly in—
>
> (a)  Not asking before he sailed for the position of our submarines.
> (b)  Assuming from a course and from a silhouette at night that the submarine sighted was an enemy.
> (c)  Not challenging before firing when there was uncertainty.
>
> All Commanding Officers of submarines are being informed of this incident and of the mistakes made.[8]

In May, 1940, the French submarine *Antiope* attacked her sister ship *Sybylle* off Terschelling. *Antiope*, *Sybylle* and *Circe* had all sailed from Harwich on 16 May, 1940, for a patrol off the Dutch coast. The submarines proceeded indpendently to their respective patrol areas. Shortly after surfacing on the evening of 19 May *Antiope*'s look-outs sighted a submarine about 4000 yards away to the south. The moon was full and *Antiope*'s Commanding Officer decided to

126

launch a submerged attack However, there was some debate about the identity of the target so *Antiope* closed to 2000 yards to try to establish the identity of the other submarine. When the target proceeded to the west into an unoccupied patrol zone *Antiope* surfaced and gave chase. By now *Antiope*'s officers, and the embarked Royal Navy liaison officer, agreed that the submarine was neither British nor French so three torpedoes were fired at a range of 1500 yards at 0056 on 20 May.

All three torpedoes missed: one passed ahead, the other passed astern and the third went unobserved. The submarine *Antiope* had attacked was the *Sybylle* which was badly out of position and was proceeding slowly on the surface re-charging her batteries. Until *Antiope*'s torpedoes were seen to pass ahead and astern she was unaware that she was being followed. The third torpedo roared underneath *Sybylle* and was clearly audible, to the great consternation of those inside the submarine. The Commanding Officer of the French submarine flotilla at Harwich concluded that:

> The Commanding Officer's (of *Antiope*) conviction that the submarine was a U-boat was based upon its apparent colour and the fact that he could see no gun armament. At night all kinds of mistake are possible and the Commanding Officer of *Antiope*, who is very keen, was lacking in prudence in attacking a submarine at night when he knew the disposition of Allied submarines.[9]

Another example of such an incident involved the British submarines *Clyde* (Lieutenant Commander D. C. Ingram RN) and *Truant* (Lieutenant Commander H. A. V. Haggard RN) on 22 July, 1940. At 2236 on 22 July *Clyde* was on the surface in position 58°30'N 02°45'E when another submarine was sighted to the NW against the light. Ingram's first reaction was to dive and carry out a submerged attack but the visibility was insufficient so *Clyde* was brought back to the surface but kept well trimmed-down with her forward casing submerged. The "target" was 30° on *Clyde*'s port bow. When the range came down to 1500 yards Ingram fired a salvo of six torpedoes at eight-second intervals. Ingram's patrol report continues:

127

I dived as the third torpedo was being fired and, as no explosions indicating a hit were heard, I commenced to reload the salvo and stalk the submarine by HE which was clearly audible. Some nine minutes later six violent explosions told of the torpedoes striking the sea bed. Shortly after this ASDIC impulses were heard on 10kc/s and I transmitted the submarine identification letter. Pendants of HMS *Truant* were then heard on SST ... I then surfaced, sighted *Truant* and carried out the challenge and reply procedure, after which I proceeded on passage.[10]

Why had not Ingram made the challenge before attacking? His decision, cogently argued in his patrol report, was based on intelligence given to him before he departed on patrol to the effect that U-boats were active in his area and that therefore he should remain dived by day. Consequently when *Clyde* surfaced on the night of 22 July for the daily battery charge Ingram was very much on the qui vive in the hope of sighting a U-boat. He knew that *Truant* would be passing through his patrol area but believed that she was much further along on her route than she actually was. Ingram's calculations placed *Truant* some seventy miles further away. He concluded:

I was so sure that the submarine was not *Truant* that I decided not to throw away all chance of a successful attack by making the challenge.[11]

Commenting on the incident Captain (S) 9th Submarine Flotilla noted that:

The position of a submarine on passage to or from patrol can rarely be accurately known or definitely forecast; and in this case the independent reckonings made in the staff office of Vice Admiral (S) and Captain (S) 9th Submarine Flotilla materially agree with the Commanding Officer HMS *Clyde* in estimating HMS *Truant* much further ahead than in fact she was. The

128

Commanding Officer of HMS *Clyde* was particularly keyed up to the probability of encountering a U-boat in the area under consideration, and the realization of this "atmosphere" makes this incident perfectly understandable.

Complete surprise encounters between our own submarines have not been frequent during the present war but are liable to increase in number with the ever growing number of submarines employed. It is clear that more stringent precautions must be imposed to protect our own submarines even though this operates to the advantage of the U-boats.

This incident ended fortunately for HMS *Truant* though it must be regretted that, had the target been a U-boat, it would not have been sunk.[12]

This incident, and the preceding one involving the *Sybylle* and *Antiope*, amply illustrate the difficulties facing Commanding Officers when they know that friendly forces are in the area. It is a dilemma which has never been satisfactorily resolved: should one challenge and risk throwing away an opportunity, or should an attack be mounted without making the challenge and risk attacking a friendly ship?

In the Atlantic there were few submarine vs submarine incidents which is remarkable considering the nature of convoy battles where several U-boats would be manoeuvring in a close tactical situation with no means of communicating with one another other than by visual signalling by which time it might be too late. Few British submarines were employed on operational patrols in the Atlantic. As the range of aircraft and availability of anti-submarine craft increased, British submarine patrols in the Atlantic and Bay of Biscay were discontinued because their presence was both unnecessary and undesirable. From the spring of 1942 onwards British submarines used the Atlantic solely as a route to and from the Mediterranean and the Far East. The submarine HMS *Clyde*'s last patrol in the Atlantic, however, was the occasion for an incident (her second such encounter) which could have had tragic results. *Clyde* (Lieutenant Commander D. C. Ingram RN) was engaged in screening the oiler RFA *Dingledale* in February, 1942, when she encountered a submarine on the surface. *Clyde* had already found the area to be a fruitful one for U-boat operations (including a hair-raising encounter with *U-111* and *U-68* on 28 September, 1941) and Ingram was taking no chances. He dived and fired two torpedoes which missed, just as the "U-boat" was identified as a British R-class submarine. The boat was HMS *Regent* which was heading for Punta Delgado in the Azores to effect repairs to storm damage.

There is no record of one U-boat torpedoing another during an Atlantic convoy battle. However, as the German official history noted:

> The danger always existed during large convoy battles that other U-boats attacking at night could not be seen.[13]

In fact there were two such instances of collisions between U-boats operating in close company on the surface at night. Although they are not strictly instances of friendly fire, they are included because at the time the collisions took place the submarines were operating in a close and rapidly developing tactical situation.

In December, 1942, the *Draufgänger* and *Panzer* wolf packs, a total of twenty-two submarines, were operating against the UK-bound convoy HX. 217. On the night of 8 December *U-254* (*Kapitän-Leutnant* Odo Loewe) was rammed by *U-221* (*Kapitän-Leutnant* Hans Trojer). The latter sustained relatively little damage but *U-254* sank immediately and only four of her crew could be picked up by *U-221* on account of the bad weather. A subsequent enquiry found that in no way could Trojer be held responsible but that in future no more than thirteen to fifteen U-boats should be in the vicinity of a convoy at any one time so as to keep the risk of collision within reasonable limits.[14] Five months later, on the night of 3/4 May, 1943, *U-439* and *U-659* collided with each other and sank while both submarines were engaged in following a convoy off Cape Finisterre.

At the end of April, 1943, a patrol line of U-boats, named *Drossel*, was ordered to take up position on an east-west line whose

130

centre lay about 475 miles west of Cape Finisterre. Among the nine U-boats ordered to form this line were *U-439* (von Tippelskirch) and *U-659* (Stock). The former had only recently left Brest when she received the signal and did not have to make a large alteration of course to reach her allotted position at the western end of the line.

Early on the morning of 3 May the *Drossel* pack received orders to proceed at full speed to intercept a south-bound convoy which had been reported by one of *Fliegerführer Atlantik*'s Fw. 200 reconnaissance aircraft at a position about 275 miles to the east of them. Soon after they had started another southbound convoy was reported not far from the first one. The convoys were bound for Gibraltar from the United Kingdom. The first consisted of fifteen Motor Torpedo Boats escorted by the trawlers HMS *Bream* and HMS *Coverley*; the other was "Landing Craft Flight D" and consisted of twenty-eight landing craft escorted by the trawlers HMS *Huddersfield Town* and the Norwegian *Molde*. At 0800 on the morning of 3 May the MTB convoy was about 250 miles to the north-west of Cape Finisterre with the landing craft convoy about fifty miles ahead on its starboard bow steering a parallel course. The landing craft were doing seven knots as opposed to the MTBs' ten knots so during the night of 3/4 May the landing craft were slowly overtaken. The two convoys were then about ten miles apart.

To reach the convoys the U-boats had to make a voyage of about 300 miles on an east-south-easterly course. Von Tippelskirch decided to attack the MTBs while Stock considered that the larger slower landing craft would make a better target. Both commanders were well aware that if they failed to find their chosen target the other convoy was not too far away. All through 3 May the U-boats chased after the convoys. About 2300 on 3 May *U-439*, having crossed ahead of the landing craft convoy, came up astern of the MTB convoy. She worked around the convoy and by dawn on 4 May she was shadowing from a position four miles ahead.

However, *U-659* was having less success in finding the landing craft convoy. She must have got close to it but had failed to sight the low-lying craft, but instead had gone so far across its track that by 0125 she was ahead of the MTB convoy. Stock had no idea of

131

where either convoy was and, believing that he had fallen behind, altered course to the south and started to pound ahead in the rough sea leaving both convoys astern of him.

Meanwhile another of the *Drossel* boats attacked the MTB convoy and the first lieutenant of *U-439*, who was on the bridge as OOW and who, "by nature was lazy and easy going,"[15] became so intent on watching the display of starshell on his port quarter that he, and everyone else on *U-439*'s bridge, neglected to watch the port bow which was his sector to watch and where it was possible to see *U-659* getting closer and closer. Von Tippelskirch now came onto the bridge and ordered a slight alteration of course to port.

The two submarines did not merely collide. *U-439*, travelling at seven knots, rammed *U-659* which was travelling at full speed, in the control room. Oil and water poured into the submarine's hull through the gash and moments later a large wave swept over the submarine sending her to the bottom. Stock and his first lieutenant had been on the bridge when the collision occurred and had gone below to make sure that all the crew got out. However, in doing so they stayed below too long and were trapped together with the engine room staff and the telegraphists who had stayed at their posts doing their duty to the end.

After the collision *U-439* went astern with the result that, in the heavy sea running, her diesel exhausts were blocked and the boat quickly filled with fumes. At the same time she began taking water into the torpedo stowage compartment in the bow which had to be closed off. Von Tippelskirch ordered the bow tanks to be blown to restore trim but they had also been damaged. He then ordered the after tanks flooded but this made the boat so low in the water that it rapidly became clear that she would have to be abandoned. Big waves were now breaking over *U-439* and her end was the same as *U-659*'s only minutes earlier. A particularly large wave swept over her from astern and she disappeared. The conning tower hatch was shut at the time so she may well have drifted just below the surface for a while: the crew trapped inside her may have survived her for a short time but they would not have been able to blow the tanks to surface the submarine. Possibly HMS *Coverley* finished off the submarine for she reported striking a submerged object in the area two hours later.

At about 0300 *MTB. 670,* which was leading the starboard column of the MTB convoy, ran into diesel smoke and fumes and saw men swimming in the water. She picked up twelve men in all: nine from *U-439* and three from *U-659. U-439*'s first lieutenant, knowing that his negligence was responsible for the disaster, had refused offers of a lifebelt and, clutching the conning tower rail, went down with his submarine.[16]

Though the French Navy was no longer involved in hostilities following the armistice of July, 1940, the presence of units of the Vichy French Fleet at sea posed problems for both British and German forces. Ships of the Vichy Navy were permitted to move from base to base after the permission of the permanent Franco-German Armistice Commission at Wiesbaden had been obtained and were supposedly immune from the hostile attentions of either side. The routes used by French units were notified to British and German forces in advance so that misunderstandings did not arise. However, the system did not always work.

On 19 December, 1940, *U-37* (*Korvetten Kapitän* Nicolai Clausen) was on patrol off the Canary Islands when he sighted a submarine proceeding on the surface escorted by a tanker. Believing the ships to be British, Clausen attacked both and was rewarded with a hit on the submarine. Alas the submarine was the Vichy French *Sfax* which was on passage to West Africa escorted by the tanker *Rhone.* Though not strictly an incident of friendly fire, the *Sfax* should have been immune from attack since she had been given permission by the Joint Franco-German Armistice Commission to move from the Mediterranean to French West Africa. However, the German submarine had not been informed, or had not received the signal informing U-boats already at sea of *Sfax*'s movements.

The confined waters of the Mediterranean, where British, French, Italian and German submarines were operating, would appear to be a fertile area for such incidents. Surprisingly there were few, largely because the various "embargoes" appear to have worked. Nevertheless, the Italians lost one submarine and Britain nearly lost another. On 19 September, 1940, the Italian submarine *Serpente* (*Capitano di Corvetto* Vittorio-Emmanuele Tognelli) attacked the submarine *Colonna* off Santa Maria di Leuca at the entrance to the Adriatic but the torpedoes missed. However, on 8 October there was a much more serious incident. The three submarines *Gemma* (*Capt. Corv.* Guido Montezemolo), *Tricheco* (*Capt. Corv.* Alberto Avogadro de Cerrione) and *Ametista* were ordered to set up a patrol line off the Caso Channel at the eastern end of Crete. The submarines were disposed to the north, south and middle of the channel to catch any British shipping landing troops and supplies in Crete. On 7 October, 1940, the *Tricheco* had been given permission to finish her patrol and return to base at Leros. In doing so she passed through the patrol area occupied by *Gemma*. When de Cerrione sighted another submarine on the surface at 0121 on 8 October he did not consider the possibility that the submarine might be *Gemma* occupying her rightful patrol area. De Cerrione fired two torpedoes and saw both of them hit. There were no survivors from *Gemma*. This was a dreadful error of sheer carelessness by *Tricheco*'s Commanding Officer. *Gemma* had been sunk for two reasons: firstly that *Tricheco*'s Commanding Officer did not make himself familiar with the disposition of friendly forces in the area and secondly that he made no attempt to confirm the identity of the target before firing.

On 12 February, 1941, the British submarine HMS *Upholder*, commanded by Lieutenant M. D. Wanklyn RN, had just completed exercises with the destroyer HMS *Havock* before heading for her patrol area off Tripoli in North Africa. Early in the evening when just 25 miles south of Malta, another submarine was sighted on the surface. Wanklyn had not been informed of any friendly submarine movements, so prepared to deliver a full salvo of six Mk. VIII torpedoes. Wanklyn was evidently unsure of the identity of the other submarine for, although he had ordered the torpedoes to be brought to the ready, he remained on the surface and closed to within 2,000 yards, even though this meant that his own submarine could be framed in the other boat's torpedo sights.

The challenge was signalled four times using a signal lamp but no reply was received. Eventually Wanklyn made his mind up, "No, that's a T-class; leave it alone". Wanklyn's intuition and excellent night vision had saved the other submarine, HMS *Truant* (Lt Cdr H. A. V. Haggard RN) from almost certain destruction.

134

But what was *Truant* doing in the safe channel outside Malta, unannounced? It later came out that Haggard had decided to return to Malta earlier than anticipated after a long and action-packed patrol in which the wireless transmitter had broken down. He was therefore unable to inform the authorities at Malta that he was on his way back. Commander George Simpson, Commanding Officer of the famous 10th Submarine Flotilla at Malta, endorsed Haggard's decision and noted Wanklyn's "good judgement" in breaking off the attack. Although he concluded that the pyrotechnics attending the nightly air raid over Malta probably distracted the lookouts on *Truant*'s conning tower, he noted that:

> to fail to see four challenges from about one mile is inexcusable.[17]

The next incident also involved two British submarines and is of note in that both participants were dived at the time. On 8 August, 1941, the British submarine HMS *Talisman* (Lt M. Willmott RN) left Malta for direct passage to Alexandria. At 1040 on 14 August *Talisman* was dived and "heard", using her hydrophones, the noise of another submerged submarine. *Talisman* turned to follow up the contact and attack and by 1253 the range had come down to 800 yards. *Talisman* fired a salvo of three torpedoes, but none was heard to explode, although they all ran correctly. After the attack *Talisman* remained in contact until dusk when the other submarine surfaced. Willmott was not to be deprived of his target so surfaced and chased after her hoping to engage the other submarine with his 4" gun. However, before *Talisman* could come within range she was sighted by the other submarine who fired the correct recognition signal. *Talisman* responded correctly and a nasty incident was thus avoided for the submarine was HMS *Otus* which was on passage from Alexandria to Malta.

*Otus* (LT R. M. Favell RN) had left Alexandria on 13 August in company with HMS *Taku*. *Talisman* was due in Alexandria on 15 August and, since there was a risk of her meeting *Otus* and *Taku*, she was routed well to the south and the west of them. *Otus* and *Taku* were warned of *Talisman*'s route but, due to a large amount of signal traffic between Malta and Alexandria, *Talisman* had not

135

been told that two Allied submarines would be in the area. There lay the root of the matter, but the subsequent analysis also revealed that *Talisman* was as much as ten miles off track when the incident occurred.

On the other side of the world there was one submarine vs submarine engagement which would have had the most far-reaching diplomatic consequences had the details been known at the time. The Japanese submarine *I-25* (Lt Cdr M. Tagami IJN) arrived off the coast of Oregon on the west coast of the United States for a patrol which was to include two raids on local forests by the submarine's light aircraft armed with incendiaries. By the middle of October, 1942, she was on her way back to Japan with only one torpedo left when on the morning of 11 October one of her lookouts reported masts on the horizon. *I.25* dived and Tagami identified the ships as two submarines proceeding on the surface. Understandably he assumed that the submarines were American and fired his remaining torpedo which scored a hit, sinking one of the submarines.

Unfortunately the submarines were not American but Soviet. The submarines *L.15* and *L.16* were proceeding from Vladivostok to Murmansk via Panama but only *L.15* arrived at San Francisco on 15 October. She reported that *L.16* had sunk as a result of an internal explosion on the 11th and this explanation was accepted until the American postwar investigators were able to analyse Japanese operational papers when the true fate of *L.16* became known. Although Russia was at war with Germany at the time, she remained scrupulously neutral as regards Japan, since Stalin did not want to be engaged on two fronts simultaneously. However, the diplomatic consequences of this incident can be imagined.

The Americans went to great lengths to prevent fratricide amongst their submarines and, by and large, were successful. All the principles of deconfliction were rigidly adhered to and, apart from some air vs submarine incidents early in the war when, understandably, everyone was fairly jumpy, American submarines could get on with the war without worrying about the attentions of their own side. The Americans were also aided by a highly centralized system of control of submarine operations which meant boats were kept away from one another while on patrol.

The risks of fratricide increased when American industry began to turn out submarines at a huge rate and the number of boats in theatre increased rapidly. The introduction of "Wolfpacks" in 1943 added another complication with the vision of a number of boats operating in close company in a tactical situation. Fears were real and pungently expressed by many submarine commanding officers. In the event their worst fears were never realized, largely due to the excellent nature of tactical communications provided by the VHF "TBS" (Talk Between Ships) radio which allowed the pack commander immediate and unrivalled control over the boats in his group. However, although the highly centralized American way of running submarine operations worked to prevent fratricide, even the best laid plans can go awry.

In the spring of 1944 the USS *Lapon*, a *Gato* class submarine[18] under the command of Lieutenant Commander L. T. Stone USN, was on her fourth war patrol in the South China Sea. After an attack on a Japanese convoy off Saigon on 24 May, 1944, in which two ships were sunk, Stone received the exciting news that a Japanese submarine was operating in his patrol area. In the next patrol area, due south of *Lapon*'s, was the USS *Raton* (Lieutenant Commander J. W. Davis USN). After sinking the Japanese *Kaibokan* type escort *Iki* on 24 May, the same day that *Lapon* was carving up the convoy, Davis headed north and in doing so approached *Lapon*'s area.

On the morning of 27 May *Lapon* was 200 miles south-east of Saigon, proceeding dived but making frequent sweeps with the large search periscope. At 0503 the boat was galvanized into action:

> Sighted submarine identified as enemy on base course about 035°. Determined it to be of the I-68 class as found in ONI-14.
> 0504  Turned away for a stern tube attack.
> 0513  Fired first of two torpedoes at a range of 1400 yards, track 53° port. Before firing the last two torpedoes the previous certainty that this was an enemy submarine was lessened in the mind of the Commanding Officer and fire was checked.

0518    Heard two explosions of torpedoes exploding at
        the end of their runs.[19]

Meanwhile *Raton*, which was on the surface, had been experiencing some mutal interference on her SJ-type surface radar set, indicating that another set of the same type, and therefore another submarine, was nearby.

0615    Ship shaken up considerably by either two
        underwater explosions or by striking sub-
        merged object. People in forward torpedo room
        thought we had struck something or been
        struck by something. Commanding Officer was
        in control room at the time en route to the
        bridge and it appeared to him to be two heavy
        muffled explosions nearby on the port side.
        Went hard right and steadied on course 035°T
        (at the time of the explosion we were on course
        350°T going ahead full on three main engines,
        17 knots).[20]

Stone did not attempt to contact the other submarine which he had belatedly recognized as American and Davis remained blissfully unaware of the identity of his assailant. It was only when both boats had returned to Fremantle in Western Australia (*Lapon* on 6 June, *Raton* on 23 June) and the staff had time to study the respective patrol reports, that the matter was resolved. The positions for the attack given by both submarines checked within two miles and the timing was almost simultanenous.

This was the only such incident in the US Submarine Force which is remarkable considering the large number of US and Japanese submarines employed in a theatre which contracted rapidly as the war progressed. It is testament to both efficient staff work and good training in and implementation of recognition procedures by a thoroughly professional body of officers and men.

The last such incident during the war took place off the Norwegian coast and involved two British submarines: HMS *Tapir* (Lt Cdr J. C. Y. Roxburgh RN) and *Turpin* (Lt Cdr J. S. Stevens

RN). The incident had some parallels with the *Lapon/Raton* affair, since it was interference from a radar set fitted to both submarines which provided the means of identification. Both submarines had recently been fitted with the new Type 267W surface warning radar set which gave greatly improved coverage over the Type 291 set previously used. *Tapir* and *Turpin* went out on patrol together in April, 1945, occupying adjoining billets off the Norwegian coast and great things were expected from the new radar set. As it turned out 267W proved to be *Turpin's* salvation.

On the night of 6 April, 1945, *Tapir* picked up the HE (hydrophone effect) of another submarine. *Tapir's* Commanding Officer, now Vice Admiral Sir John Roxburgh, recalled that:

> We heard him surface so I immediately broke surface to get my 267 on it. I got a lovely blip on it so I tracked it very quickly with my standards sticking up about 5 or 6 feet to get a picture.[21] He was going away at speed so I surfaced to chase him and was about to overtake him, but he was about to leave my area and go into Stevens' who was patrolling next door. I wasn't going to catch up with him so I got ready to send an enemy report when suddenly to my astonishment I got the correct challenge from the other side immediately followed by "Don't shoot, Steve here!"[22]

*Turpin* had found herself out of position so had surfaced to proceed to her area at speed. Her 267W operator had detected *Tapir* coming up astern so Stevens reduced speed to assist the development of a range and bearing plot. It was only when *Turpin's* 267W operator reported mutual interference from a similar 267W set that Stevens realized that the other submarine could only be *Tapir*. On this occasion the correct procedures worked. *Tapir* did not go out of her area and the correct challenge and reply were given. Nevertheless *Turpin* had a lucky escape for had *Tapir* come within range Roxburgh would have undoubtedly fired. Six days later Roxburgh despatched U-486 (*Oberleutnant zur See* Gerhardt Meyer) in the same area.

As a footnote to this chapter it is worth looking at an incident

139

in the 1956 Suez Crisis. The British submarine HMS *Tudor* (Lt W. G. Edwards RN) was assigned to air sea rescue duties together with the French submarine *La Créole*. During the operation *La Creole* gained a sonar contact while dived with another submerged submarine. The target was assessed as hostile for although the Egyptian Navy possessed no submarines there were a number of Soviet boats in the area, together with an American boat which was making a nuisance of itself. *La Créole* began to manoeuvre for a firing position and in accordance with the ROE (Rules of Engagement) then in force *La Créole* reported her intentions to the Force Commander. Fortunately *La Créole* was ordered only to fire in self-defence since the other submarine was HMS *Tudor* regaining her patrol position following a navigational error.

# CHAPTER TEN

## *Submarines vs Ships*

The Court Martial is waiting for you.

*Message awaiting Kapitän-Leutnant Peter Cremer of U-333 on return from patrol, February 1942.*

Submarine vs ship engagements represent the smallest category of friendly fire incidents at sea. Submarines operated alone, separated (hopefully) from even their own kind and it was highly unusual to have surface forces operating in areas where submarines were on patrol. This state of affairs only ever existed in the Pacific where so-called Joint Zones were established. In such an area a target could only be attacked once it had been positively identified as hostile.

On 15 April, 1940, the British submarine HMS *Taku* (Lieutenant Commander V. J. H. van der Byl RN) was on patrol at the entrance to Fro Havet near Trondheim in Norway. The following day she was ordered to move south in order to clear the area for friendly surface forces who were carrying out a sweep along the coast. It therefore came as no surprise to van der Byl when he sighted the distinctive shapes of two Southampton class cruisers, HMS *Glasgow* and HMS *Sheffield*. However, van der Byl had not been warned that British destroyers were in the area. On the other hand, information was received that five German destroyers had been seen off Stavanger at 1900 on the 16th. A quick look at his chart told *Taku*'s Commanding Officer that the German ships would pass through his patrol area at about 0330 on the 17th. At

0335 a ship was sighted about four miles off and proceeding at high speed. Seven minutes later van der Byl fired a salvo of four Mk. VIII torpedoes at a range of 3,000 yards. All four torpedoes missed. The destroyer ran down the tracks to deliver a depth charge pattern. Before going deep van der Byl had recognized his target as British (she was, in fact, the Tribal class destroyer HMS *Ashanti* commanded by Commander W. G. Davis RN) and decided to surface rather than take his chances with a second pattern. Fortunately, as *Taku* broke surface in front of an alert and angry destroyer, *Ashanti*'s Director Layer (the rating responsible for setting the master sight in the director on the target) recognized the distinctive silhouette of a T-class submarine and her pendant number N-38, and ordered cease fire.

*Ashanti* was in the area to join the cruisers *Calcutta, Effingham* and *York* who had been ordered to find the same force of German destroyers which *Taku* had been warned about. In retrospect it was unwise to despatch surface forces to an area in which friendly submarines were operating for the same purpose, but caution may have been overridden by operational necessity. Van der Byl could be forgiven his error in recognition: through a periscope a *Tribal* class destroyer did bear a superficial resemblance to a German destroyer especially if the latter is what he was expecting to see. To commemorate the incident, which was accepted with good humour by both parties, Commander Davis had a scroll fixed to *Ashanti*'s bridge screen on which was embossed Jack Warner's famous catchphrase, "Mind my Bike!"

Over a year later on the morning of 21 March, 1941, the British T class submarine HMS *Tetrarch* (Lieutenant Commander R. G. Mills RN)) was en route to Alexandria in rough weather with short steep seas, after a patrol off Tripoli which had been notable for the number of mechanical defects rather than anything else. At 0320 the OOW sighted an object at a range of two miles, which was identified as the conning tower of a submarine. *Tetrarch* made the challenge *five times* without receiving a reply during which period the range came down to 2,000 yards and the target turned through 180°.

At this point Mills judged it inadvisable to delay firing any longer since his own submarine was dangerously exposed.

142

Accordingly a full bow salvo of six Mk. VIII torpedoes was fired. When no hits were registered, the 4-inch gun's crew were closed up, but before the order to commence firing was given, a round was mistakenly fired, which also missed. Tetrarch was now just a cable's length away and the "submarine" was identified as a coaster, the auxiliary schooner *Zingarella,* a captured Italian vessel, which was on passage from Sollum to Alexandria and under the command of an engineering officer from *Tetrarch*'s depot ship!

Captain S. M. Raw, Captain (S) First Submarine Flotilla, was not best pleased at the waste of six valuable torpedoes:

> At night these small schooners bear a marked re-
> semblance to a submarine trimmed down, and this
> mistake in identity is easy to understand. Having
> decided to his own satisfaction that the target was a sub-
> marine the Commanding Officer was right to fire a full
> salvo of six torpedoes. The fact he considered it neces-
> sary to challenge, however, indicates that he was not so
> certain and the target's action in turning rather than
> diving while the challenge was being made should have
> cast further doubt in his mind. I consider therefore, that,
> having in mind the possibility of meeting small craft off
> Alexandria the judgement of the Commanding Officer
> was at fault and that, before wasting six valuable tor-
> pedoes, he should have further closed the range and
> established the identity of the target with reasonable
> certainty.[1]

The two most important losses from submarine v. ship attacks affected the German *Kriegsmarine* and both concerned blockade runners. Throughout the Second World War the Germans enjoyed considerable success in running merchant ships from the Far East to the French Atlantic port of Bordeaux. The ships would sail inde-pendently, relying on disguise, bad weather and luck to see them through the British blockade. The blockade runners were vital ships for not only did they carry strategically important cargoes such as tin, rubber, quinine and wolfram, unobtainable from within Germany or from any of her possessions, but they often carried personnel of the German merchant marine who had been interned abroad on the outbreak of war. The German Navy needed every trained seaman it could lay hands on to keep the U-boat fleet manned. Lastly the ship herself was a valuable asset. No wonder the sailing and routing of blockade runners was done with great care and their safe arrival a matter for some ceremony.

The Hamburg-Amerika Line's *Spreewald* had managed to reach the safety of Yokohama on the outbreak of war, before being interned at Dairen (formerly Port Arthur). However, in 1941 she was brought back to service and loaded with rubber, quinine and wolfram for return to Germany. *Spreewald* left Dairen on 21 October, 1941, and while at sea embarked 300 British prisoners from the German supply ship *Kulmerland*. These were survivors of the ships sunk by the German raider *Kormoran*. Using a number of disguises *Spreewald* began her long voyage and by January, 1942, she was on the final approach to Bordeaux and safety.

Also on patrol was *U-333*, a Type VIIC U-boat commanded by *Korvetten-Kapitän* Peter Cremer (whom we last met as the gunnery officer of the unfortunate *Theodore Riedel*). *U-333* was Cremer's first operational submarine command and he was keen to do well. So far his patrol had been moderately successful with three ships totalling over 12,000GRT to his credit. At 1516 on 31 January, 1942, a steamer was sighted at a range of 5,000 to 6,000 yards. *U-333* dived and Cremer went to within 350 metres of the freighter to determine her nationality:

> Definitely enemy ship: a zig-zag general course which would lead to Ireland. A British ship with slim masts, no cross trees, only found on British ships. One gun at the stern. No neutrality marks, no flag.[2]

To be absolutely sure, Cremer asked his first lieutenant to confirm his identification since "two men see more than one". At 1648, satisfied that he was attacking an independent steamer or a straggler from a convoy, Cremer fired one torpedo which hit the ship amidships. Cremer then intended to surface and finish off the cripple with gunfire, thus saving his last torpedo. However, when his telegraphist reported that the ship was broadcasting her position *en clair* on the 600 metre distress frequency, he abandoned this plan and used his last torpedo. Before firing however, he asked the boat's quartermaster, (*Obersteuerman*) and coxswain (both experienced merchant seamen) to verify his identification (although at this stage it was a bit late) and both confirmed that in their opinion the ship was British. The second torpedo was fired at 1833 and the ship subsequently sank, burning furiously. Meanwhile Cremer had sent a delighted signal to U-boat command announcing that in square BE7100 (using the *Kriegsmarine*'s grid map of the Atlantic) he had sunk a large passenger-carrying freighter.

Cremer's signal was recieved at Kerneval, the French head-quarters of Admiral Dönitz, after the distress call sent out by the merchant ship. At first she had used her false name, that of the British Royal Mail Line steamer *Brittany*, but later came clean and announced that the German ship *Spreewald* was sinking and appealing for assistance. It didn't take long for the staff at Kerneval to realise that *Spreewald* had been sunk by *U-333*. Cremer was blissfully unaware of the furore he was causing for he could not receive the *Spreewald*'s last signal. It was only when he was ordered to join the rescue operation which involved nine boats, including *U-333*, that the identity of his target dawned on him. Only twenty-four of the crew and fifty-eight prisoners were rescued by *U-105*.

On Cremer's arrival at the port of La Pallice, near La Rochelle, there were none of the festivities which usually marked a return from patrol. There was just a grim-faced staff officer to whisk the unfortunate Cremer away to a court martial to face a charge of, "Disobedience in action, manslaughter and damage to military property". In the end Cremer had nothing to worry about. The court found that the *Spreewald*, was running ahead of schedule and that she had not sent a routine signal advising the German com-mand of her route. Presumably the master of the *Spreewald*, having got thus far, did not want to compromise his position with a radio transmission. Accordingly the U-boat assigned to escort her, *U-575*, could not be in the right area to meet her. Likewise, none of the other boats at sea were informed that a blockade runner was homeward bound because nobody knew where she was. Conse-quently, when *Spreewald* was sighted by *U-333*, Cremer identified her as what her master had disguised her to be: the British steamer

145

*Brittany*. Cremer's career did not suffer from this incident. He was awarded the Knight's Cross in 1942 and, after being badly injured in a surface gun duel with a British corvette, he joined Dönitz's staff, where he remained for the rest of the war, although appointed to command *U-2518*, a Type XXI submarine.

A week before the loss of the *Spreewald*, another blockade runner slipped quietly out of Bordeaux and headed for Japan. The ship was the 5154GRT *Doggerbank* which had been the British ship *Speybank* until taken over by the Germans on the outbreak of war. *Doggerbank* arrived in Batavia sometime in the summer of 1942 and commenced loading her cargo of 7,000 tons of crude rubber from Malaya, together with mineral, vegetable and fish oils from Japan. On 17 December, 1942, she left Kobe and headed for home. On 3 March she was sighted off the Canary Islands by *U-43* commanded by *Kapitän-Leutnant* Hans Joachim Schwantke. Schwantke identified the ship as British, possibly the *Dunedin Star*; in any case he had not been warned of any homeward-bound blockade runners. Accordingly he sank her and then surfaced to close the few lifeboats that had got away. Unfortunately he failed to confirm his victim's identity as darkness had fallen and he was ordered to join a new patrol line.

Twenty-six days later the Spanish tanker *Campaomor* came across one man virtually unconscious in a dinghy of Japanese origin. The man was Fritz Kurt, a seaman from the *Doggerbank* and the sole survivor of the fifteen men including *Kapitän* Paul Schneidewind, the *Doggerbank*'s Master, who had escaped the sinking. Kurt had somehow kept himself alive by catching rainwater and eating raw flying fish which had landed in the dinghy. He was landed in Venezuela and when recovered from his ordeal told a horrifying tale of how, one by one, the others had died of hunger, dehydration or had just given up. *Kapitän* Schneidewind, the Master of the *Doggerbank*, had shot four of the survivors who were critically ill, before taking his own life.[3] The Germans investigated this, the second sinking of blockade runner in fifteen months, and found that in all likelihood a signal sent to the *Doggerbank* in February and ordering her not to cross the Equator before 5 March could not have been received. Had the signal been received it is inconceivable that Schneidewind would have disobeyed it.

146

In the Mediterranean, on 8 June, 1942, the Italian submarine *Alagi* (*Teniente de Vascello* Sergio Puccini) attacked and sank the destroyer *Antoniotto Usodimare* in error. *Usodimare* had left Naples at 0200 on 8 June as escort to the liner *Pisani* which was carrying troops to North Africa. By 2125 the two ships had entered the Sicilian Channel and were in company with another convoy. The entire force was sighted by the *Alagi* which had not been warned of friendly shipping movements. Puccini fired a "browning" salvo at the formation and one of his torpedoes struck the *Usodimare* amidships. The destroyer was travelling at speed and she broke in half and foundered extremely quickly. Fortunately none of Puccini's other torpedoes found a target.[4]

This chapter closes with an incident, the only one of its kind, in the Pacific theatre, in which the USS *Extractor* was mistaken for a Japanese I-Class submarine with fatal results. On 23 January, 1945, the USS *Guardfish* (Commander D. T. Hammond USN) was returning to Guam when at 2038 a radar contact was made with a ship steering 270°, 11,000 yards away. *Guardfish* was operating in a Joint Zone, an area where both surface ships and submarines operate but where they are forbidden to attack one another unless positive identification of the target as hostile was made. In this case Hammond couldn't be sure: it didn't look like an American ship and she was not using any known American radars. However, he lacked information on current friendly ship movements in the area so sent a contact report and requested further information. This was followed by a signal to ComSubPac (Admiral Charles Lockwood at Pearl Harbor, commander of all US submarines in the Pacific) repeated to Commander Task Group 17.7 at Guam, giving the target's course and speed and indicating his intention to attack when sure that the ship was Japanese.

At 0113 on 24 January ComSubPac replied that no friendly submarines were in the area but that, as *Guardfish* was in a Joint Zone, the ship was probably American. A quarter of an hour later a signal was received from Commander TG. 17.7 which ordered *Guardfish* to stay in contact. This was followed at 0338 by a second signal from Guam which, while reminding Hammond that he was in a Joint Zone, informed him that the area was clear of all friendly forces.

This was enough for Hammond and by 0542 he had positioned *Guardfish* 13,600 yards ahead of the target and 2000 yards off track. This would silhouette the target against the early morning sun and allow positive identification to be made. At 0605 the target was identified as a Japanese I-165 class submarine and this was confirmed by Hammond and his Executive Officer. Fifteen minutes later Hammond fired four Mk. 18 electric torpedoes at a range of 1,200 yards. Two hit but, as the stricken ship's stern rose as she took her final plunge, Hammond saw with horror that it was not another submarine that he had just sunk. *Guardfish* was brought to the surface where seventy-three survivors of the USS *Extractor*, a salvage ship, were rescued, six of her crew having died in the sinking.

The inevitable Board of Enquiry found that Commander TG. 17.7 at Guam had no idea that *Extractor* was in the area. On the previous afternoon *Extractor* had been ordered to return to harbour. However, the signal was so garbled in transmission that it was unreadable when received. *Exctractor*'s Captain was unwilling to break radio silence to request a repeat, so continued on his course. Meanwhile the staff at Guam thought he was heading back on a reciprocal course. Consequently when *Guardfish*'s request was received, the port director merely noted that *Extractor* had been ordered to return, thereby clearing the area, without actually checking that the signal had been received and acted on. Consequently he felt able to confirm to *Guardfish* that the area was clear.

The Enquiry took no action over the staff on Guam whose fault was that they had done their duty but no more. They came down far harder on Commander Hammond. He was judged to have acted improperly on a number of counts: firstly in that he did not use underwater telephone (UWT) equipment fitted in his submarine which could have been used to communicate with *Extractor*. In his defence Hammond argued that there was no evidence that *Extractor* was fitted with the UWT and that he, along with many other sub-mariners, regarded the equipment as dangerous since the Japanese could home in on its transmissions. This was not accepted. Secondly the Enquiry concluded that Hammond had relied on visual identification only, making six periscope observations of the

148

target at various angles on the bow (between 15° and 50°). The Enquiry felt that firstly the periscope observations were carried out at a time when visibility was not good and that secondly Hammond viewed the target from an angle on the bow which was far too fine. Had the angle been nearer to 90°, then it would have been much easier to identify the submarine.

The Enquiry acknowledged that Hammond did not fire in haste and that he had acted in good faith on intelligence supplied by higher command. Nevertheless they laid down that the burden of identification rests on the submarine commander, particularly in a Joint Zone and for this reason Hammond was given a formal reprimand, which was the end of his career in submarines.

# CHAPTER ELEVEN

## *Self-Inflicted Lossess*

I really think it looks remarkably like one of ours.

*Captain J. Saunders RN of HMS* Trinidad *on seeing one of his own
torpedoes coming back on its track, 29 March, 1942.*

The most literal form of friendly fire is the malfunction of weapons.
It is debatable whether such incidents should be included in a
survey such as this, but since they cause casualties and material
damage, they merit inclusion. On 8 May, 1941, the battlecruiser
HMS *Renown* was screening the eastbound *Tiger* convoy to Malta.
In the evening an air attack developed which focused on *Renown* as
the main target. Enemy hits on the *Renown* were avoided by skilful
ship-handling. Unfortunately in the course of the action, the inter-
ceptor release gear on P3 twin 4.5" failed. The turret was thus able
to train further round than would normally be allowed and two
shells went into the back of P2 mounting, killing five of the crew
and wounding twenty-eight.

The torpedo is the main culprit in respect of malfunction. A torpedo's delicate gyro mechanism could be easily upset with serious
consequences. Rogue torpedoes were an occupational hazard for
submariners and there are dozens of instances where a submarine
was forced to dive deeply to avoid one of her own torpedoes which
was coming back.

One of the most dreadful accidents involving a torpedo occurred
on board the French destroyer *Maille Breze* on 30 April, 1940,
while at anchor at the Tail o' the Bank on the Clyde. Her torpedo

tubes were trained facing fore and aft when at 1415, during routine maintenance, one of the torpedoes was accidentally fired into the rear face of the forward superstructure. The air vessel exploded and the ship was consumed by fire, aggravated by sympathetic explosions of ready use ammunition on the upper deck. Despite valiant efforts by the ship's company aided by civilian fire fighters, *Maille Breze* gradually filled with water and sank. Flag Officer in Charge Greenock reported that there were two dead, twenty-three missing and ten badly wounded.[1]

The cruiser HMS *Trinidad* was another such victim of a rogue torpedo when she was damaged while escorting convoy PQ. 13 to Russia in March, 1942. On 29 March, following bad weather, the convoy was split into two groups which were about eighty miles apart with four ships whose whereabouts was unknown. The westerly group of eight ships was being escorted by HMS *Eclipse* (Lt Cdr E. Mack DSC) and the trawler *Paynter* (Lt R. H. Nossiter DSC RANVR). At 0645 on the 29th they were reinforced by HMS *Oribi* and two Soviet destroyers. At 0843 the cruiser *Trinidad*, with the *Fury* in company, were steaming east to collect the easterly group of four ships and bring them back to the other group when *Trinidad*'s radar picked up a contact bearing 079° at a range of 6. 5 miles. Six minutes later the German destroyer *Z.26* came in sight almost right ahead. *Trinidad* immediately turned to starboard to open her "A" arcs and opened fire at a range of 2,900 yards. *Z.26* took violent avoiding action and, although being hit, managed to seek the safety of the mist. *Trinidad* manoeuvred to avoid any torpedoes which the destroyer might have fired and at 0922 she fired one at *Z.26* which had reappeared and was seen to be on fire. The torpedo appeared to be running true but two others failed to leave their tubes due to icing. Meanwhile *Trinidad* was still pounding the unfortunate *Z.26* with 6" shell and all was going well, when at 0923 a torpedo broke surface 200 yards off *Trinidad*'s port bow. Although the wheel was put hard over to port, it was too late and the torpedo struck on the port side. The explosion ruptured the wing tanks below the bridge and flooded the Marines' messdeck, almost cutting off the men in the Transmitting Station (the fire control centre for the ship's 6-inch armament). Four escaped before the armoured hatch fell back breaking the back of the fifth. Almost

151

simultaneously the bulkhead separating the compartment from the breached oil tank gave way and the seventeen men remaining below were drowned in the filth of heavy fuel oil. Water poured into the forward boiler room and, amid the super-heated steam escaping from fractured steam mains, men were badly burned as they tried to escape. The ship rapidly assumed a 17° list to port and her speed fell to 8 knots.

After being struck by the torpedo *Trinidad* had turned to the SE and was steering 130° at six knots when she was rejoined by HMS *Fury*. Speed was cautiously increased and at 1100 the western group of merchant ships was overhauled. Captain Saunders ordered the *Oribi* to join his screen and early in the afternoon HMS *Harrier* joined the screen. By this time good damage control had succeeded in reducing the list so that the ship now lay on an even keel and was making between 12 and 14 knots. Late that night, however, salt water contamination of the boiler feed water forced the ship to reduce speed to 2 knots and threatened to stop her altogether. A signal was sent to SBNO North Russia requesting tugs and air cover, but by 0200 on 30 March her speed had increased to seven knots. By early morning the wind had increased and was blowing hard from the northward with a considerable sea. Once the ship broached to and had to go astern in order to bring her stern into the wind and head to the proper course. Tugs were met but their assistance was not required and at 1230 *Trinidad* anchored at Rosta.

The story of *Trinidad*'s torpedoing had a curious sequel. On the 7 May, while the cruiser was still under repair at Murmansk, a stoker discovered a part of a torpedo pistol while clearing wreckage from "A" boiler room. The item was speedily identified, by its markings and shape, as coming from the torpedo fired by *Trinidad* during the engagement with Z.26. *Trinidad* had undoubtedly been struck by her own torpedo which had gone back on its track. A Board of Enquiry subsequently convened at Plymouth found that the torpedo had not been prepared for cold-water running since the necessary oils had not been available. A number of technical possibilities for the torpedo's malfunction were examined but in the end it seemed likely that the intense cold had caused the engine and gyro oil to freeze. No blame was attributed to *Trinidad*. As Admiral Sir John Tovey, the Commander in Chief Home Fleet, put it in his report, it was "cruel, hard luck".[2] Alas, for *Trinidad* there was more cruel, hard luck in store for she was sunk on 14 May, 1942, while returning to the UK. In a similar incident the German *Schnellboot S.26* was sunk in the Black Sea on 5 September, 1942, when a torpedo fired at a Soviet transport off the Taman Peninsula came round and sank its originator.

The problems suffered by the United States Navy with its torpedoes during the Second World War are well documented. But aside from the immense amount of Japanese shipping which avoided destruction on account of torpedo failures, two American submarines were lost – sunk by their own torpedoes which failed to run true. The USS *Tullibee* (Commander Charles F. Brindupke USN) had left Pearl Harbor on 5 March and, after fuelling at Midway, departed for her patrol area on 14 March. Her orders were to go north of Palau where she was to pariticipate in operation *Desecrate*, an attack by carrierborne aircraft on Palau planned for 30 March. She was not heard from again and was formally declared lost on 15 May, 1944. There the matter rested until the end of the war when an emaciated Gunner's Mate 2nd Class C. W. Kuykendall was liberated from the Ashio copper mines in Japan. Kuykendall was the only survivor from *Tullibee's* crew of eighty officers and men and naturally he was subjected to a thorough debriefing from staff of the Submarine Force as to what had happened to his submarine.

He told of how, on the night of 26 March, he was on lookout duty on the bridge when contact was established by radar with a convoy of a troopship and three freighters escorted by a destroyer and two A/S vessels. Visibility was poor with frequent rain squalls: twice Brindupke began an attack only having to break off on account of the driving rain. On his third attempt he drove through the screen, who were by now aware of his presence and were dropping random depth charges, and fired two torpedoes at the troopship. Kuykendall was peering through his binoculars waiting for the explosion when the submarine was rocked by a tremendous explosion and he was thrown into the sea. As he struggled to remain afloat, Kuykendall could hear the shouts and cries of other survivors in the darkness around him. He stayed afloat throughout the night and was picked up the next morning by a

Japanese escort. Kuykendall was certain that the Japanese had not sunk the *Tullibee*. The ranges and bearings of the three escorts put them out of position for a successful counter-attack. The only other conclusion was that one of the two Mk. XIVs' fired at the transport suffered a failure of its steering gear and circled back to strike the *Tullibee*.

The problems associated with the Mk. XIV torpedo and the associated Mk. VI exploder are well documented. Less well known is that the Mk. XVIII electric torpedo[3] was another such weapon which often malfunctioned and on one occasion did so with disastrous consequences. The US Navy had developed an electric torpedo following the capture of a German G7e torpedo of the same type. The electric torpedo offered a number of advantages over the wet-heater engine torpedoes in that they were extremely cheap and quick to produce and, once running, left no tell-tale wake in the water. However, the weapon gave endless problems as related in the Official History of US submarine operations:

> The first ones taken to sea lacked hydrogen burning circuits and therefore had to be frequently withdrawn from the tubes for ventilation. Several instances of hydrogen explosions and fires occurred. One fire on board the *Flying Fish* heated the warhead until the torpex melted and ran. There were some erratic runners, slow runners and sinkers. The torpedoes' tail vanes were found to be weak and had to be strengthened. Cold water and low battery temperatures caused the torpedo to run slow and several misses were due to this unforeseen obstacle. Hot runs in tubes following depth charging were caused by the failure of the guide studs. Warping of the thin shell of the battery compartment resulted in binding in the tubes.[4]

The worst such failure of a Mk. XVIII resulted in the loss of the USS *Tang* (Lieutenant Commander Richard H. O'Kane USN), a *Balao* class fleet submarine with a displacement of 1826/2414 tons, on 25 October, 1944, in the Formosa Straits. *Tang* had left Midway on 27 September, 1944, for her fifth war patrol. O'Kane was an extremely experienced Commanding Officer who had commanded *Tang* since her commissioning in 1944 and who had learned his trade as executive officer to the famous "Mush" Morton of USS *Wahoo*. Under O'Kane's command *Tang* had sunk seventeen Japanese merchant ships totalling 116,454 tons in four patrols.

*Tang*'s fifth patrol was set to be as successful as the others. O'Kane chose the area between the north-west coast of Formosa and the China coast for his patrol: a focal point for Japanese shipping but also an area which was bounded by minefields to the east and an enemy coast to the west. On the night of 10/11 October O'Kane sank the *Joshu Go* and *Oita Maru* and on the 23 October sank a further three vessels (*Toun Maru, Wakatake Maru* and *Tatsuju Maru*) in a fiercely fought convoy action.

Twenty-four hours later contact was established with another convoy steaming south to support the Japanese forces engaged in the Philippines. The decks of the tankers and freighters were piled high with crated aircraft. O'Kane decided to attack on the surface and drove through the screen launching two torpedoes at a tanker and four at two transports. Fired at a range of less than 1000 yards, the six torpedoes hit as planned with a series of violent explosions. *Tang*'s position was revealed by the light of the exploding ships and she was virtually boxed in by merchant ships and escorts converging from all sides. A large troopship and a tanker were astern of her, a destroyer was coming at her from one side while two *Kaibokan*-type escorts came in from the other. Three burning ships were ahead of the submarine. O'Kane ordered full speed to clear the area while at the same time firing on the tanker, the transport and the closing destroyer:

> There was but one priority, to get the hell out of here and this time I blessed the great blotch of smoke from our four diesels, for it received a well-placed large-calibre salvo from the DE. Other escorts now directed their fire our way and my enquiry revealed that Frank was pleading with Culp for more turns. Successive blotches of smoke told of the nature of Frank's request. I could almost hear the words, "To hell with overload and smoke, pour on the coal!"

Only seconds had passed but never had smoke taken a tougher beating from large and small calibre fire. We were grateful but not laughing, for the DE was still plowing toward us. The single torpedo had hit home in the tanker, and the fire changed the whole area to an evening twilight. I considered clearing the bridge since we now had no after torpedoes to shoot. The decision was made unnecessary by two tremendous explosions astern, one in the transport and the other completely obliterating the DE.[5]

Once clear of the convoy, the torpedomen loaded the last two Mk. XVIIIs into the forward tubes, carrying out the complicated preparation routines, a procedure which took about an hour. During this period O'Kane held *Tang* at a safe distance from the convoy while maintaining a watch on a stricken transport using his SJ surface-search radar.

At 0125 on the morning of 25 October O'Kane took *Tang* back to finish off the troopship. The escorts were patrolling to seaward of the ship and allowed *Tang* to slip in from the landward side. At 0230 the range was down to just under 1,000 yards and the first torpedo was fired. The second torpedo, *Tang*'s last, was fired shortly afterwards but instead of running true, broke surface made a sharp turn to the left and began to porpoise off *Tang*'s port bow while turning in toward the submarine.

O'Kane now attempted to take his submarine outside of the errant torpedo's turning circle. The helm was put over to starboard followed by a turn to port in an attempt to swing the stern clear of the warhead. But it was to no avail. The torpedo bore in relentlessly and struck *Tang* on the port side abreast the after torpedo room and close to the manoeuvring room bulkhead:

Our stern went under before those of us topside could recover from the blast. One glance aft told me that there would be insufficient time to clear the bridge ahead of the sea. My order "Close the hatch" was automatic, and my heart went out to those below and to the young men topside who must now face the sea.

156

Our ship sank by the stern in seconds, the way a pen-
dulum might swing down in a viscous liquid. The seas
rolled in from aft, washing us from the bridge and
shears, and of small consolation now was the detonation
of our 23rd torpedo as it hit home in the transport.[6]

Of the nine officers and men on the bridge at the time the torpedo
struck, three, including O'Kane, swam throughout the night and
were picked up eight hours later by a Japanese patrol boat. A fourth
officer managed to escape from the flooded conning tower and
stayed afloat by an ingenious conversion of his trousers to a
lifejacket.

Inside the submarine the explosion of the torpedo was very
violent, breaking HP air lines and lifting deck plates. Many of the
crew sustained fractures from being violently thrown to the deck.
The after torpedo room, manoeuvring room and after engine room
were flooded immediately and none of the crew escaped from these
compartments. It had been impossible to shut the upper hatch on
the bridge and the lower hatch was leaking badly, so the remaining personnel, thirty officers and men, made their way to the
forward torpedo room, carrying the wounded in blankets, to prepare
for an escape. Despite repeated depth charge attacks from Japanese
escorts, the escape began at 0600, nearly four hours after the submarine had sunk. However, only thirteen of the remainder actually
escaped from the submarine. It is believed that the remainder were
asphyxiated by fumes from an electrical fire and the burning of confidential books or a battery explosion. Of the thirteen who escaped,
five clung to *Tang*'s indicator buoy and were picked up, three others
reached the surface but subsequently drowned and the remaining
five were not seen after leaving the escape trunk.[7] Seventy-eight
officers and men of the *Tang* were killed.

The nine survivors endured the rigours of Japanese captivity and
were liberated at the end of the war. Lieutenant Commander
O'Kane was awarded the Congressional Medal of Honor and the
submarine was awarded a second Presidential Unit Citation, one
of only two US submarines to receive such a distinction. But it was
cruel irony that one of her own torpedoes had ended the career of
such a successful submarine.

A third US submarine may also have been the victim of one of her own torpedoes. The USS *Growler* (Commander Thomas B. Oakley Jr USN) was sunk on 8 November, 1944, off Mindoro in the Philippines in position 13° 53'N, 119° 26'E. Two possibilities exist to account for her loss, but neither has sufficient evidence to permit a definete conclusion to be drawn. *Growler* had left Fremantle in Western Australia for her eleventh war patrol on 20 October, 1944. On 8 November she was attacked by the Japanese destroyer *Shigure* and escort vessels *Chiburi* and *No. 19*. The Japanese made their attacks in their usual desultory manner and there was no visible result: no claim was made for a submarine sinking. Distant "observers" to *Growler*'s ordeal were the submarines *Hake* and *Hardhead* which were occupying neighbouring patrol positions. Both heard the depth-charging on their passive sonars, but *Hardhead* also heard the detonation of a torpedo.

The introduction of the acoustic homing torpedo provided new complications. The British and Americans introduced "Fido", an acoustic homing torpedo, in May, 1943: for security reasons the device was known coyly as the Mk. XXIV mine.[8] Fido's guidance was based on four passive hydrophones. When dropped into the water from an aircraft Fido went to a preset depth and began an acoustic search for the submarine, the detection range being 1500 yards. If nothing was "heard" the torpedo began a circular search pattern which was maintained for up to fifteen minutes. The weapon was first used by US Navy TBM Avenger torpedo bombers operating from escort carriers in the Atlantic and its first success was the sinking of *U-266* on 14 May, 1943, by a VLR Liberator of 86 Squadron RAF.

However, during trials, one disadvantage of the weapon came to light. The hydrophones could not distinguish between the cavitation noises of a U-boat and those from a friendly escort. Moreover, the peculiar nature of sound propagation under the sea meant that the theoretical detection range of 1500 yards could be exceeded. On one occasion the escort carrier HMS *Biter* was chased by a Fido when the carrier entered the torpedo's detection range while the torpedo was "hunting", thus leading to the celebrated crack to the effect that "thus was the *Biter* bit!"[9] On a more serious note, the threat of a Fido running amok amidst an escort group or

158

convoy was a situation which no one particularly cared to contemplate. Therefore restrictions had to be placed on the release of the weapon when friendly forces were in the vicinity.

A little later the *Kriegsmarine* introduced their own acoustic homing torpedo, the T. 5 *Zaunkönig* (*Wren*), better known as the *Gnat*, German Naval Acoustic Torpedo. It was first employed in September, 1943, and was intended to be a counter to the effective close defence of convoys by the escorts. Using a T. 5 meant that a U-boat commander need not get so close to a convoy and its escorts but could fire and simply wait for the torpedo to pick up a target.

At least two U-boats are known to have fallen victim to their own T. 5s. In January, 1944, *U-377* (*Oblt. z. S* Gerhard Kluth) and *U-382* (*Oblt. z. S* Rudolf Zorn) were engaged in operations north of the Azores where the American carrier group, TG. 21. 16 was operating in support of GUS (Gibraltar-USA, slow) and UC (UK-Caribbean) convoys. On 14 January *U.382* was depth-charged by the destroyers USS *Bulmer* and *Parrott* and then depth-charged by a B. 17 of 206 Squadron RAF Coastal Command. She was able to dive and eventually returned to Wilhelmshaven where she was damaged beyond repair in an RAF raid in January, 1945.

*U-377* is often given as the victim of one of these attacks, but this could not be so for twenty-four hours later, at 0404 on 15 January, she reported having unsuccessfully attacked TG. 21. 16 with a T. 5. Shortly after that signal a further message, with a corrupt signature, was received by U-boat Command to the effect that the originator had been hit by a torpedo, was badly damaged and was sinking. The signal was sent on the *Diana* frequency, one of three frequencies used by U-boats when engaged in operations, and therefore the signal had to come from a U-boat. *U-377* was never heard from again which was unusual; given that since the boat was in contact with a task group it would have been reasonable to expect further situation reports from her. Since there is no evidence to link any other boat with the signal, it is most likely that the originator was *U-377*.

The second such U-boat to be sunk by a T. 5 is *U-869*. The circumstances of her loss are unclear but the recent discovery of her wreck with a gaping hole by the submarine's control room, the area from where the most noise would be emanating when the boat was dived, would seem to indicate that a rogue T. 5 was responsible.

The mine was another weapon which was absolutely indiscriminate. It is almost impossible to say with any accuracy how many ships were destroyed by mines laid by their own side, given that mines could break free from their moorings and drift, and that the same waters were mined by both sides. Two simple examples will suffice: on 23 March, 1917, the British destroyer *Laforey* entered a British minefield in the Channel and was sunk, while on 14 March, 1942, *U-133* (*Kapitän Leutnant* Hemer Hesse) struck a mine in a newly laid German field off Salamis and was sunk.

However, the worst instance of ships running into one of their own minefields was that which befell convoy QP. 13, returning from the Soviet Union in June, 1942. This story has been overshadowed by that of the eastbound convoy, PQ. 17, but the story of QP. 13 is no less tragic. This convoy of thirty-five ships had sailed in two parts from Murmansk and Archangel and had joined up at sea on 28 June under Commodore N. H. Gale. The escort consisted of five destroyers, an anti-aircraft ship, four corvettes, two minesweepers and two trawlers.

The convoy had an uneventful passage. Although it was reported by the *Luftwaffe* on 30 June and 2 July while east of Bear Island, it was left unmolested, the Germans concentrating on PQ. 17. On 4 July the convoy divided off Iceland with sixteen ships under Commodore Gale turning south for Loch Ewe while the remaining nineteen headed around the north coast of Iceland to Reykjavik with Captain J. Hiss, Master of the US freighter *American Robin*, as Commodore. At 1900 on 5 July the convoy was approaching the north west corner of Iceland in five columns escorted by the minesweepers HMS *Niger* (Commander A. J. Cubison as senior officer) and *Hussar*, the Free French corvette *Roselys* and two trawlers. The weather was bad, with visibility down to less than one mile, with rough seas and the wind coming from the north-east at Force 8. Due to bad weather it had not been possible to take star sights since 2 July and the convoy's position had been calculated by dead reckoning and was therefore considerably in doubt.

At 1910 Cubison suggested to Hiss that the convoy's front be reduced to two columns in order to pass between the Straumnes and the minefield to the north-west of Iceland. Soon afterwards Commander Cubison gave his estimated position at 2000 as being 66°45'N, 22°22'W. and suggested altering course to 222° to clear Straumnes Point. This was done. Two hours later *Niger*, which had gone ahead to make a landfall, leaving *Hussar* as a visual link with the convoy, sighted what she took to be the North Cape bearing 150°, one mile, and ordered course to be altered to 270°. What *Niger* had actually sighted was an iceberg and the alteration of course to the north had the effect of taking the convoy directly into the minefield they were trying to avoid. At 2240 *Niger* blew up and sank with heavy loss of life, including Commander Cubison. Just before striking the mine Cubison had realized his error and had signalled to Captain Hiss, recommending a return to a course of 222° and explaining the mistake.

It was too late. As Hiss looked around him, explosions were occurring all over the convoy as ships ran into mines. In the reduced visibility six ships struck mines: *Exterminator, Heffron, Hybert, Massmar* and *Rodina* sinking and John Randolph being damaged. The escorts displayed conspicuous gallantry in entering, or remaining in, the minefield to rescue the survivors. The conduct of the French corvette Roselys (*Lieutenant de Vaisseau* A. Bergeret) was particularly noteworthy. Although Bergeret appreciated that the convoy had blundered into a minefield, he kept his ship in the highly dangerous waters for six and a half hours during which time he rescued 179 survivors. Finally a definite shore fix was obtained by *Hussar* and the remaining merchant ships reformed and reached Reykjavik on 7 July without further misfortune.

Flag Officer Iceland (Rear Admiral Dalrymple-Hamilton) conducted an enquiry into the affair and concluded that the main cause had been *Niger*'s navigational error which had been compounded by the bad weather that had prevented sights being taken for three days before landfall. He also commented on the fact that Captain Hiss, who had taken over as Commodore after QP. 13 split, had not been provided with full information about defences NE of Iceland. Hiss was unaware that a minefield existed in these waters. Hamilton also recommended that a DF beacon be installed to help ships make a landfall in these treacherous waters.

The most tragic form of friendly fire is when casualties occur when an enemy ship, properly attacked, was subsequently found to contain prisoners of war or refugees. One such example was the 15,501GRT *Arandora Star* torpedoed on 2 July, 1940, by *U-47* (*Kapitän-Leutnant* Gunther Prien). *Arandora Star* was sailing independently because of her high speed and was carrying 1,178 German prisoners of war and Italian aliens being transported to Canada. 613 of the transportees were killed, as well as ninety-one guards and fifty-seven of the ship's crew.

In the Pacific, in a similar incident, an American submarine "Wolfpack", consisting of *Growler, Pampanito* and *Sealion* named "Ben's Busters" after Commander Ben Oakley of *Growler*, encountered a six-ship Japanese convoy on the night of 11/12 September, 1944, en route to Japan from Singapore. Oakley had been warned of the convoy by signals intelligence but all the intelligence in the world could not have told him that 1,350 British and Australian PoWs were crammed into the *Rakuyo Maru* and the *Nankei Maru*. "Ben's Busters" tore into the convoy. In their first attack two escorts and the two PoW-carrying freighters were sunk: two more ships were subsequently sunk before the remnants took refuge in the Hainan Straits.

On the afternoon of the 15th *Pampanito* (Lt Cdr Paul E. Summers) re-entered the area where the first attack had taken place and discovered, amid the debris, a crude raft loaded with men. As *Pampanito* moved through the debris she began to find more groups of men holding on to makeshift rafts or swimming in the oil-covered water. They were the British and Australian survivors who had been abandoned by the Japanese rescue ships who had picked up their own men while keeping the prisoners in the water with rifle and pistol fire. They had all been nearly five days in the water on top of suffering the effects of nearly three and half years of Japanese captivity and were in a pitiful condition. Summers signalled to *Sealion* to join him and both submarines picked up seventy-three and fifty-four men respectively but could then take no more. Their submarines were full to well above capacity. Further help was on the way when *Barb* (Lt Cdr Eugene G. Fluckey USN) and *Queenfish* were diverted from patrol in the Luzon Strait and rescued another eighty-two before bad weather forced them to break off.

162

Lastly, in the confused situation in the Baltic at the end of the Second World War the German merchant ships *Thielbek* and *Cap Arcona* were sunk by RAF Typhoons while at anchor in Neustadt Bay. The ships were part of what was known as the *KZ-Häftlings-Flotte* (Concentration Camp Prisoner Fleet) and had been employed in evacuating concentration camp inmates from the east. As the amount of German-held territory shrank, it was decided to use the ships as floating concentration camps. The purpose of the ships had been declared to the Swedish Red Cross but this information was not forwarded to the Allied command. At this stage in the war the Allies were determined to prevent the flight of the German government to Norway (or anywhere else) and so engaged on a ruthless campaign of destroying all transport assets wherever they could be found. There was no way that the staff at 84 Group RAF could have known that these two ships were packed with the sick and dying inmates of the former concentration camps of Neuengamme, Stutthof and Auschwitz-Birkenau. On 3 May, 1945, the ships were attacked by rocket-firing Typhoons of 197, 198 and 263 Squadrons. In a series of attacks from 1415 onwards. *Thielbek* sank within fifteen minutes and *Cap Arcona* was left a blazing wreck. The number killed will never be known but at least 8,000 were killed outright, drowned or were shot, having reached the shore, by German soldiers or the SS. That the prisoners, whose sufferings were already beyond belief, should have met their end at the hands of their liberators when they must have known that the end to their tribulations was so near is one of the greatest tragedies of the Second World War.

# CHAPTER TWELVE

## *Which Way Forward?*

The lines between opposing forces are anything but clear and the
fog of war rapidly descends even when matters are proceeding
more or less as intended.

*Rear Admiral John Woodward, 1982*

The postwar period has seen naval development dominated by the
electronics revolution. This was already foreseen at the end of the
Second World War with old ships being hurriedly modified to take
on board an avalanche of new gadgets. None of this equipment has
made the task of identifying a potential target any easier, IFF
having failed to live up to expectations despite constant upgrad-
ing and development. The recent shooting down of two American
Black Hawk helicopters over Iraq only goes to prove that even the
most sophisticated electronic systems do not make the problem of
recognition any easier. In fact the problem has got worse.

Modern radar systems can detect targets at ranges undreamed of
during the Second World War. The naked eye's limit of vision is
to the horizon, which can vary according to the level of visibility.
With the sorts of search radar current in 1945 this level could be
increased to over the horizon, giving much better warning of
impending attacks. Today the maximum detection range is
hundreds of miles, particularly when aircraft fitted with Airborne
Early Warning (AEW) are used. When combined with the development of long-range missiles such as Exocet and Harpoon and
their various stablemates in the former Soviet arsenal a potent combination has been forged.

Navies now have the ability to detect, lock-on to and engage a target hundreds of miles away without having made visual confirmation that the target is friendly or not. Speaking of the land battle casualties from friendly fire in the 1991 Gulf War, General H. Norman Schwarzkopf noted that, "our technological ability to engage targets exceeded our ability to identify targets clearly".[1] Although the General's comments related to the land battle, they are equally pertinent when applied to the war at sea.

A missile homing in on the target indicated to it by its homing radar is delightfully indiscriminate. It does not recognize friend or foe: it sees only targets. In 1968 the American cruiser *Wainwright* fired an anti-radar missile against an air defence radar in North Vietnam. The missile malfunctioned, searched around for another target and found *Wainwright.* The cruiser was badly damaged and her superstructure was reduced to a shambles. The Argentine pilots who released the Exocet missile against HMS *Sheffield* on 4 May, 1982, had no idea of what they were firing at. The target could have been one of the two British carriers or it could have been something smaller. It could have been a neutral merchant ship meandering through the British carrier battle group. They had no way of knowing. On the other side the Royal Navy nearly shot down a Brazilian airliner believing it to be, on the basis of radar information, an Argentine snooper. It was only last-minute visual identification by a Sea Harrier that prevented a tragedy on a scale equal to that of the shooting down of the Korean Air Lines 747, and a diplomatic incident with terrific ramifications. Electronics have not helped in finding a solution to the problem of friendly fire.

A further complication has been the spread of weaponry and sensors made by "first world" countries to nations in Latin America, the Indian sub-continent and South-East Asia who are all intent on expanding their forces and who invariably have some festering territorial dispute with a neighbour. There is an awful lot of weaponry and sensors, which has either been purchased or provided under an aid scheme, in simultaneous service with a number of nations, some of whom are locked together in disputes. In the purely visual field this poses problems, since both sides have the same equipment which looks the same: for example both Greece

165

and Turkey received the same type of ship from the US Navy. This was one example of both sides having the same equipment which was to have fatal consequences.

Duality also has ramifications in the electronics field. In the clash of titans between the United States and the former USSR, identification would have been simplified because each side used radars and sonars with distinct signatures that could be easily identified by Electronic Warfare (EW) specialists. However, for countries engaged in conflict who have equipment purchased from the same supplier, the situation is very different. For example, in the 1982 Falklands War both Britain and Argentina had Type 42 destroyers deployed in the South Atlantic. Since both the British and Argentine ships had the same radar fit, unless one knew the physical disposition of the ships, how was one to know whether a Type 909 transmission (the fire control radar for the Sea Dart SAM system) came from HMS *Glasgow* or ARA *Santissima Trinidad*?

However, the postwar period has not been entirely dominated by electronics. There have been a few incidents the causes for which are depressingly familiar to anyone who has read this far. During the Anglo-French operations to regain control of the Suez Canal in 1956, (Operation *Musketeer*) HMS *Jamaica* was leading the Support Group from Malta to Port Said. During the passage radar contact was gained with a group of five ships at a range of 18 miles which were approaching. Visibility was poor and thus a maritime patrol aircraft summoned from Malta to take a look at the ships could not identify them. When the range dropped to 10,000 yards the challenge was made and no reply received. However, as the ships did not appear to be hostile the challenge was repeated for twenty minutes using increasingly brighter lights. Eventually a reply was received from a group of five auxiliary French minesweepers.

Flag Officer Flotillas (Mediterranean), who was flying his flag in *Jamaica*, commented that:

> I destroyed the signal I had drafted in case they proved to be British: it would have hurt more than a few rounds of 6-inch.[2]

166

The Vietnam War provided a number of incidents, particularly air to sea ones, which can only serve to stress the value of visual recognition procedures. 16 June, 1968, was a bad day for US Navy/US Air Force relations. South of the De-militarized Zone (DMZ) PCF-19 was bombed and sunk by a USAAF F-4 Phantom jet. Five men were killed and two wounded. The investigation found that the pilot had acquired the target on radar and attacked it without making visual identification, believing it to be a helicopter. He did not say why he thought it necessary to attack a helicopter given that such a craft would surely be either American or South Vietnamese. A little later on that day, the cruiser USS *Boston* and destroyer HMAS *Hobart* were also attacked by F-4s. *Hobart* sustained two killed and seven wounded. There is no explanation for this incident. No visual identification was carried out. What the pilot thought he was firing at has not been made clear: North Vietnam had nothing in her naval inventory that even approached the size of either the *Boston* or the *Hobart*.

During the Turkish invasion of Cyprus in July, 1974, aircraft of the Turkish Air Force sighted a *Gearing* class destroyer south of the island. Believing this to be a Greek ship (Greece and Turkey having received *Gearing* class destroyers from the United States) bringing reinforcements to the island, they attacked and sank her. The ship was the Turkish destroyer *Kocatepe.* In this case the problem was compounded by both sides having the same equipment. Visual identification was carried out by the aircrew, but the wrong conclusions were drawn.

The Royal Navy had evidently learned from this lesson, for at the time of the 1982 Falklands War British Type 42 destroyers wore a large black identification stripe down each side, stretching from funnel to waterline in order to make them clearly distinguishable from their Argentine counterparts.

In the same conflict the landings at San Carlos posed some problems for the organization of the air defence of the landing force. With every Sea Harrier virtually worth its weight in gold, the prospect of one being shot down by the air defence at San Carlos was not one which too many British planners wished to contemplate. Accordingly Rear Admiral John Woodward, the Carrier Battle Group Commander, allocated an area ten miles across and two miles high which covered all of San Carlos and the eastern shore of Falkland Sound from North West Island to Fanning Head. British Harriers were banned from entering the box. British helicopters would be allowed in the box but were to get out of the way during an air raid and were not allowed out.

The advantages of this arrangement were that the missile aimers and gunners on board the British warships and transports had *carte blanche* to shoot at any fixed-wing aircraft inside the box without bothering about the niceties of identification. This was critical in view of the speed at which an Argentine air attack developed. At a speed of 400 knots an Argentine Mirage would traverse the box in 90 seconds, hardly any time at all for a gunner armed with a 7.62 GPMG.[3] If the Argentines wanted to attack the landing ships then they would have to endure the gunfire and missile barrage in the box and when they emerged at the other side the Harriers would be waiting for them. Likewise any helicopter outside the box could be treated as hostile and engaged by either the Sea Harriers or SAM-armed ships.

It was a beautiful plan, elegant in its simplicity. As Admiral Woodward wrote:

> It also might have seemed a bit primitive, but simplicity is the only sensible policy when fast reactions are required in confused situations involving three different services.[4]

The arrangements only failed once. Early in the morning of 6 June the Type 42 destroyer HMS *Cardiff* (Captain M. Harris RN) was ordered to conduct a bombardment of Port Stanley with HMS *Yarmouth* (Commander A. Morton RN). Just after 0400 *Cardiff* detected an unidentified air contact moving out of the box and heading east across East Falkland. A quick check of the signals revealed nothing to indicate any British air operations in that area that night. Under the Rules of Engagement this contact had to be Argentine, possibly a special forces helicopter heading back to Stanley. With very little time to ponder the question, Captain Harris made the only decision open to him and ordered the target to be engaged with the Sea Dart SAM. Two missiles were fired and one of them brought down the target at a range of eleven miles, just short of Mount Pleasant.

The next day one of 5 Brigade's Gazelle helicopters was announced as missing and, when the wreck was found, it was very close to where *Cardiff*'s target had been shot down. A forensic investigation found that there were no remnants of a Sea Dart with the wreckage and so the matter was closed. However, three years later a second investigation, carried out at the behest of some of the relatives, was positive that fragments of Sea Dart had been found with the wreckage.

The aircraft, Gazelle XX377 from 656 Squadron Army Air Corps, had been tasked to take signals personnel to repair a defective rebroadcast beacon on Mount Pleasant. For some reason the pilot had broken the rules and flown out of the box on a course leading to Port Stanley. We shall never know why he did it, but his breaking of the ROE, either deliberately or by accident, cost him, his aircrewman and his two passengers their lives. This tragedy was the only encounter between air and sea forces during the entire campaign which must set records for safety and organization.

However the nature of the command organization of the British forces in the Falklands led to two incidents of friendly fire between ships. Overall command of the British forces deployed in the South Atlantic was vested in Admiral Sir John Fieldhouse at his headquarters at Northwood, 8,000 miles away from the Falklands. Three commanders in the South Atlantic: Woodward (Carrier Battle Group); Thompson (3 Commando Brigade, joined later by Major General Jeremy Moore who assumed command of all land forces on the Falklands) and Clapp (Amphibious Ships) were all of roughly the same seniority. In theory any matter which affected all three had to be dealt with by the staff at Northwood who, as many of those who have written their memoirs of the campaign have testified, were not in touch (through no fault of their own) with the nature of conditions in the Falklands. There was no one commander in the South Atlantic to tie the threads of the operation together. The result was the development of a certain amount of "fog of war" caused by the multiplicity of command authorities and units in a small and complicated theatre of operations.

Just how complicated operations in the Falklands were is illustrated by the organization of operations involving land and sea forces on the night of 5/6 June, the night on which the Gazelle was shot down and on which there were three incidents involving British ships. The destroyer HMS *Cardiff* and frigate HMS *Yarmouth* were ordered to patrol off East Falkland operating under the command of the Carrier Battle Group (CTG. 317. 8) while co-operating with 3 Commando Brigade under CTG.317. 1 (Commander Land Forces Falkland Islands). However, their bombardment station was off, and they were firing over, the area occupied by another TG. 317.1 unit – 5 Infantry Brigade. The assault ship HMS *Intrepid* carrying 560 men of the Scots Guards from San Carlos to Fitzroy was passing through *Cardiff* and *Yarmouth's* bombardment area but was under the control of CTG. 317.0 (Commodore Amphibious Warfare) who was cooperating with 5 Infantry Brigade. Helicopter movements were controlled by TG. 317.0, but each Brigade controlled their own light helicopters, while *Cardiff* and *Yarmouth* enjoyed complete autonomy in the control of their helicopters for tactical purposes. The destroyer HMS *Exeter* was air warfare controller at San Carlos but *Cardiff* was ordered to interdict the approaches to Port Stanley airfield. Such a combination of threads should have been handled by a single unified command authority. Without such an authority, deconfliction could only be maintained firstly by good staffwork in the various command authorities, and secondly by good communications. The latter was not always possible in the Falkland Islands where terrain, weather and poor atmospheric conditions combined to produce a communicator's nightmare. It was amid this complicated web of movements that the three incidents happened.

The most significant operation on the night of 5/6 June was the movement of 1st Battalion, Scots Guards which were being taken from San Carlos to Fitzroy by sea in the assault ship HMS *Intrepid*. The Scots Guards were part of 5 Infantry Brigade[5] which had arrived in San Carlos on 2 June. Brigadier Tony Wilson, the Brigade Commander, was ordered to advance to Stanley along the southern axis. Wilson wanted to move forward and on 4 June, following 2nd Battalion Parachute Regiment's victory at Goose Green, had flown a company, followed by the rest of 2nd Battalion

Parachute Regiment, into Bluff Cove and set up his advance Brigade headquarters at Fitzroy. This was a bold move and came as a complete surprise to Divisional HQ who first heard about Wilson's "great leap forward" from a Royal Marine MAW (Mountain and Arctic Warfare Cadre) patrol at Winter Quarrie who sighted a Scout and a Chinook flying west to east and dropping troops at Fitzroy before returning the same way. A fire mission was called for but cancelled when the helicopters were identified as British. The problem now facing Wilson was that he had to move the two battalions of the Scots and Welsh Guards (the Gurkhas being employed elsewhere) in order to consolidate his position. Ideally the Guardsmen could have been moved in by helicopter but there were simply not enough helicopters to move 1200 men and satisfy other demands on their services. To walk, as the Marines and Paratroopers of 3 Commando Brigade had done, would take too long and would result in numerous casualties from trench foot and exhaustion. To move the men by sea would take but five hours and would result in their arriving at Fitzroy comparatively fresh, and this seemed the most practical solution.

Eventually, after a number of options had been discussed, it was decided to move the two battalions by sea on two different nights. The Scots Guards would go first in HMS *Intrepid* on the night of 5/6 June, followed by the Welsh Guards on the following night in *Fearless*. There was no suitable anchorage at Bluff Cove (nor would it, in view of the Argentine air threat, be prudent to have large and valuable ships sitting in such an unprotected anchorage in daylight) so the move would take place at night. The assault ship would go to an agreed point – Middle Island or Elephant Island were mentioned – from where the troops would go ashore in the assault ship's four LCUs (Landing Craft Utility). The assault ship would return to San Carlos to be back under the missile umbrella there by daylight. The LCUs would then have a four-hour trip to Bluff Cove at six knots.

Major Ewen Southby-Tailyour was a landing-craft specialist who had served in, and held a deep affection for, the Falkland Islands. He was deputed to lead the LCUs into Bluff Cove but on boarding HMS *Intrepid* to discuss the operation he found that plans had changed. The command had decided that, because of the risk

171

from shore-based Exocet missiles around Stanley, *Intrepid* would not be allowed further east than Lively Island. Not only would this lengthen the amount of time the troops spent in the LCUs (an uncomfortable experience at the best of times) but the LCUs would have to make a long voyage at night unsupported and without the appropriate navigational aids for such a journey. Moreover, they would be unescorted, since it was felt that the presence of a frigate might alert the Argentines to what was happening. Rear Admiral John Woodward, the Carrier Battle Group commander, had been briefed on the operation and confirmed that no British ships were allocated for bombardment duties on the south-east coastline and that the LCUs had the area to themselves.

Southby-Tailyour was not happy:

> Told the Captain, "I think the whole fucking thing stinks" and asked him to remember my words and my requests if the thing turns sour and I fail.
>
> Navigationally it will be awkward as my memory is about all I have but On! On! I suppose. Once we get going it will be fascinating and possibly great fun!
>
> Militarily it could be awkward as there will be no friendly ships on the gunline and, of course, no escorts in case we get into trouble. The Captain confirmed that any ships we see will be enemy. I asked this two or three times and was assured that we will be on our own. Not good, but at least I know where we stand. I asked for the ship recognition signal "just in case", but he does not know the one for the Battle Group ships, so could not give it to me – but then as he pointed out, there will be none![6]

*Intrepid* duly sailed and from 0230 the Scots Guardsmen began making their way down to *Intrepid*'s tank deck, dimly lit in red, and embarked in the four LCUs. The dock was flooded up and at 0430 the four LCUs retracted from the dock and proceeded. They were not to know that earlier that night the destroyer HMS *Cardiff* and frigate *Yarmouth* had detached from the Battle Group with orders to patrol the south-east coastline and conduct harassing fire against Argentine positions as appropriate. The two ships were not told that four slow-moving LCUs containing 600 infantrymen would be passing through their area.

The journey for the Guardsmen was unpleasant to say the least. No sooner had they set off than they were fired on, either by artillery ashore or bombed from the air. The records are not clear on this point. Captain Tim Spicer, the Battalion's Operations Officer, recalled:

> The boat move that night was more frightening than the whole of the Tumbledown battle. The entire battalion was jammed into four LCUs, everyone sitting on boxes of mortar and GPMG ammunition. . . . The waves were crashing over the sides of the landing craft and everyone got soaking wet.[7]

The radar in Southby-Tailyour's craft, which had been playing up all night, suddenly started to work to reveal two ships closing from astern at 20 knots. All Southby-Tailyour's intuition told him that these ships could not be Argentinian. The Argentine Navy had not shown its face outside territorial waters since the sinking of the *General Belgrano*, but on the other hand he was not going to risk the lives of 600 men and four valuable landing craft to prove a point.

However, there was little he could do: the maximum speed of an LCU was nine knots; the warships astern of him could probably do thirty knots or more. The best he could hope for was to make for shallow water and hide among the islands, exploiting his local knowledge to the full. At 0500 the four LCUs were illuminated by starshell:

> Starshell burst overhead, then we saw a frigate bearing down on us from the darkness. I grabbed one of the machine guns. I don't know what I was going to do with it.[8]

Using a tiny red light the leading warship, HMS *Cardiff*, ordered the LCUs to heave-to which they did. The destroyer then signalled

"Friend" to which Southby Tailyour replied "To which side?" Both ships then turned away and made off to the south-east at high speed. Southby-Tailyour was very angry at what had happened. The LCUs had already been spotted by someone (either radar or an Argentine OP) and fired on earlier in their voyage, but their illumination by *Cardiff* and *Yarmouth* and the subsequent retirement by the ships would have advertised their identity, mission and probable destination. No wonder Southby-Tailyour wrote:

> I feel anger and dismay at this disregard for our problem and can only speculate at the background to such perfidy and ignorance.[9]

Eventually, after over seven hours in the open LCUs, the Scots Guards were landed at Bluff Cove, soaked to the skin and with three of their number suffering from hypothermia.

They had nearly never made it at all. What had gone wrong? Clearly, from all available evidence, it would seem that there was a failure in communication between the Carrier Battle Group, responsible for the tasking of *Cardiff* and *Yarmouth* and COMAW's[10] staff at San Carlos who were responsible for the LCU operation. Clearly communication was not what it should have been. As Southby-Tailyour said, "It is a good job that someone on board the frigate knows what an LCU looks like,"[11] for had *Cardiff* opened fire with her radar-controlled 4.5" gun, then surely all 600 Guardsmen would have drowned. The incident has been overshadowed by the bombing of RFA *Sir Galahad* two days later, but offers the student much more in the way of lessons learned.

Elsewhere that night LCU F. 4 from HMS *Fearless* was having an eventful time. She had been ordered to return to San Carlos (where the shortage of landing craft was acute) under cover of darkness from Port Salvador at the northern end of East Falkland, where she had been left by *Fearless* several nights previously. At 0310 HMS *Arrow* detected an unidentified ship off the coast and opened fire with starshell. Fortunately Colour Sergeant Johnston, F.4's Coxswain managed to satisfy *Arrow* about his identify. Three hours later, just as F.4 was turning into North Falkland Sound, she was illuminated again, this time by HMS *Plymouth*, which, like HMS *Arrow*, had not been informed of *F. 4*'s voyage. It was a very relieved *F.4* which finally arrived at San Carlos. Sadly she was sunk two days later by A4 Skyhawks of the V Air Brigade.

What of the future? Efforts continue to find a fool-proof electronic means of making identification infallible. *BASIS* (Battlefield Automatic Secure Identification System) is something devised for the land battle but which may well have naval applications. It consists of a small transmitter which continually broadcasts a signal out to a range of 12 kilometres but which is only detectable, for *Sigint* purposes, at ranges up to 1,000 metres. The system is unlikely to be accepted since commanders do not relish the idea of a beacon continually advertising their position even if the enemy can only read the signals at less than 1,000 metres. The signal may also possibly interfere with some voice communications. The Royal Netherlands Navy have developed a towed pod to give underwater acoustic identification.[12] The transponder, towed behind the ship, transmits a Morse signal giving the ship's identification code. The system was originally developed for use by hospital ships and may have other applications, but is likely to be rejected on the same grounds as BASIS. Any frigate captain probably thinks his ship makes far too much noise already without towing a sonar transponder behind him. All such means are inevitably doomed to failure, since their very nature implies a transmission of some sort which could be liable to detection and enemy action.

In 1945 Commander Arthur Pitt, a British submariner who had carried out a study of friendly fire incidents for Flag Officer Submarines, wrote that:

> More than ever before it will be essential to possess a means of identifying a friend beyond visibility range, means which must be automatic, instantaneous, infallible and immune from enemy simulation and reaching out to the effective range of the weapons carried.[13]

That day has not yet come. Even with all the sophisticated gadgets science can produce, there is still no substitute for good recognition skills, for identification procedures that are easy to observe and for good staff work to achieve deconfliction. Friendly fire will never be eliminated from the battlefield, but its chances of occurring can be drastically reduced.

# Source Notes

## Chapter 1 (pp 1–13)

1 Thucydides (Ed and trans C. Sawyer): *Complete Writings of Thucydides – The Peloponnesian War:* Random House – The Modern Library, New York; 1951; VII, 22; pp. 425-6.

2 Schrader, Charles R: *Friendly Fire:* Parametres, Journal of the US Army War College; Vol XX11, No. 3, Autumn 1992; p. 452.

3 Gardiner, R. (Ed): Conway's History of the Ship, *The Line of Battle, The Sailing Warship, 1650-1840*; London, Conway Maritime Press, 1992; pp. 162-3.

4 Navy Records Society: *Fighting Instructions, 1560-1816*; London, NRS, 1971; pp. 290-1.

5 Kemp, P. K. (no relation-author): *HM Submarines*; London 1952; pp. 128-129.

6 Keyes MSS 4/30: Keyes to Rear Admiral Christian, 29 August, 1914.

7 Ibid.

8 PRO ADM137/3745: Report of the Board of Enquiry into the Loss of H. 5.

9 PRO ADM137/3745: CCBAF to Admiralty 25 April, 1918.

10 PRO ADM137/2121: Report of Proceedings of HM Submarine H. 4, 28 September 1916.

11 Halpern, Paul: *The Naval War in the Mediterranean 1914-1918*; London, Allen & Unwin, 1987; p. 339.

12 In 1925 the officially sanctioned maximum diving depth for

an L class submarine was 150 feet – the depth to which they were tested was 100'.

13  Admiral Sir Frederick Parham to Author, 17 September, 1989.

## Chapter 2 (pp 13–22)

1  Engine Room Artificer.

2  Gus Britton to Author, 7 February, 1994.

3  Gus Britton to Author, 7 February, 1994.

4  Marder, A: *From the Dreadnought to Scapa Flow vol III, Jutland and After, May 1916-December 1916*; OUP 1978; pp. 154-55.

5  Jackson MSS: Jellicoe to Jackson, 5 June, 1916.

## Chapter 3 (pp 23–29)

1  Hill, Roger: *Destroyer Captain!*; London, William Kimber, 1975; pp. 135-6.

2  PRO ADM234/369: Report of Proceedings of the Commanding Officer HMS *Eclipse*.

3  Bassett, Roland: *HMS Sheffield – The Life and Times of "Old Shiny"*; Arms and Armour Press, London 1988; p. 151.

4  Bassett, op. cit. , p. 151.

5  The Germans referred to their motor torpedo boats as *Schnellboote* or *S-Boot*. E-boat was a term used by the Royal Navy to describe any kind of German fast patrol craft.

6  PRO ADM. 234/: Naval Staff History of the Second World War; Battle Summary No. 41; *The Evacuation From Dunkirk, Operation Dynamo, 26 May to 4 June, 1940*; Admiralty 1949; pp. 36-37.

7  A refers to the use of zone time as opposed to GMT.

8  "Headache" teams were teams of German speaking officers and ratings who specialized in the interception of German tactical communications thus providing "real-time" intelligence of enemy intentions and movements.

9   PRO ADM199/437 HMS *Garth*, Letter of Proceedings, 30 November, 1941.

10  English, J: *The Hunts*; World Ship Society, 1987; p. 64.

11  Admiralty: *Preliminary Narrative of the War at Sea*, vol II, TS Copy in IWM library; para 478.

12  TBS: Talk Between Ships – VHF voice radio.

13  Roscoe, Theodore: *US Destroyer operations in World War II*: USNIP 1949; p. 437.

14  Admiralty: *Preliminary Narrative of the War at Sea*: Vol III, para. 1162.

15  Bickers, R. T.: *Friendly Fire: Accidents in Battle from Ancient Greece to the Gulf War*: Leo Cooper, 1994; pp. 87-90.

16  PRO ADM1/2346. Report of the Board of Enquiry into the Loss of *ML. 251*.

## Chapter 4 (pp 40–53)

1   Cremer, Peter: *U-333 – the Story of a U-boat Ace*; London, the Bodley Head, 1984; p. 8.

2   Admiralty: *Führer's Conferences on Naval Affairs 1940*; London 1947; p. 11.

3   MGFA: LW9: Oberst (ad) Saul: *Die Geschichte des "F d. Luft" der 9 Fliergerdivision under des IX Fliegerkorps von der Aufstellung dierser Kommandobehorder bis zur Wende der Kriegsjahre 1940/41*; p. 8.

4   BA/MA RM8/1182: *Die Beteiligung der Deutscher Luftwaffe am der Seekriegsfuhrung seit 1939: Teil D: Nordsee, Atlantik zum 1. 11. 35 bis zum Beginn der Norwegen Unterklerung, April 1940.*

5   Ibid.

6   Ibid.

7   Ibid.

8   Ibid.

9   Ibid, Führer Directive, 28 February 1940.

10  Bassett, Roland: *HMS Sheffield – The life and times of "Old Shiny"*; Arms and Armour Press, London 1988; p. 93. If

*Sheffield*'s engineer officer, Engineer Commander Bailey RN, expected any credit for the superlative performance of his department, he was mistaken. All he received was a reprimand for inadvertently making smoke!

11    Fifteen were flown off, but one returned making a successful emergency landing without jettisoning the torpedo.

12    Papers of Commander J. Stewart-Moore RN: Department of Documents, Imperial War Museum.

13    Bassett, op. cit. , p. 93.

14    Bassett, op. cit. , pp. 93-4.

15    Papers of Commander J. Stewart-Moore RN: Department of Documents, Imperial War Museum. Stewart-Moore was indulging in the well-known naval practice of using appropriate quotations from the Bible to convey a message.

*Chapter 5 (pp 54–72)*

1    *Gleaner* had been damaged by an acoustic mine and *Harrier* had been sent back to Portsmouth with engine trouble.

2    PRO ADM156/212–3 Board of Enquiry into the loss of HM Ships *Britomart & Hussar*.

3    *The Navy's Day of Shame*: Weekend, 10-14 January, 1962.

4    Ibid.

5    PRO ADM156/212–3 Board of Enquiry into the loss of HM Ships *Britomart & Hussar*.

6    John Price to author, 25 April, 1994.

7    PRO ADM156/212–3 Board of Enquiry into the loss of HM Ships *Britomart & Hussar*.

8    *The Navy's Day of Shame*: Weekend, 10-14 January, 1962.

9    PRO ADM156/212–3 Board of Enquiry into the loss of HM Ships *Britomart & Hussar*.

10    PRO ADM156/212–3 Board of Enquiry into the loss of HM Ships *Britomart & Hussar*.

11    PRO ADM156/212–3 Board of Enquiry into the loss of HM Ships *Britomart & Hussar*.

12  PRO ADM156/212–3 Board of Enquiry into the loss of HM Ships *Britomart & Hussar*.

13  Williams, J. F. : *They Led the Way – The Fleet Minesweepers at Normandy*; Jack Williams, 1994; p. 144

14  Williams: op. cit. , P. 144

15  John Price to Author, 25 April, 1994.

16  Lowe R. W. & Major J. (Eds): *The Year of D-Day, The 1944 Diary of Admiral Sir Bertram Ramsay*; University of Hull Press, 1994; p. 127.

17  Admiralty: *The War At Sea Preliminary Narrative*; Vol V; Jan-Dec 1944; paragraph 2188. London 1946.

18  Ibid.

19  PRO M057954/44

20  *Weekend*, 10-14 January, 1962.

21  John Price to Author, 15 May, 1994.

22  Papers of Captain V. A. Wight-Boycott RN, Department of Documents, Imperial War Museum.

23  Catapult Armed Merchant Ship.

24  Papers of Lieutenant Commander E. R. Barringer RNVR, Department of Documents, Imperial War Museum, 91/17/1, P. 296.

25  PRO ADM. 234/369: Battle Summary No. 22: *Arctic Convoys 1941-45*; p. 121.

26  Admiralty: Naval Staff History of the Second World War; Battle Summary No. 47 *Okinawa, Operation Iceberg, March-June 1945*; London, 1950; p. 179.

27  Brooke Geoffrey: *Alarm Starboard – A Remarkable True Story of the War at Sea*; Patrick Stephens Ltd, 1982; pp. 250-251.

*Chapter 6 (pp 73–92)*

1  Monsarrat, Nicholas: *The Cruel Sea*; London, Cassell 1953; pp. 268-9.

2  Distinguished Service Order: the most senior award for gallantry after the Victoria Cross and, in the early days of the

war, the standard "reward" for sinking a U-boat. Towards the end of the war when U-boat sinkings were routine, Commanding Officers had to make do with an OBE, Order of the British Empire, sometimes known as Other Buggers' Efforts.

3    Engine Room Artificer: highly trained senior rates who enjoy special status accruing from their technical qualifications.

4    Young, Edward: *One of Our Submarines*; London, Hart Davis, 1954; p. 53.

5    British Empire Medal: the lowest decoration available in the entire British Honours system.

6    Captain John Stevens to Author, 10 February, 1989.

7    Stevens, ibid.

8    RNSM Archives A1941/55 Lt J. B. Selwyn RNR to Captain (S) 3rd S/M Flotilla, 5 March, 1941.

9    Selwyn, op. cit. It was the usual practice to leave the Ensign flying if the boat had to dive in a hurry.

10   RNSM Archives A1941/55

11   Selwyn, op. cit.

12   RNSM Archives A1941/55: Auboyneau to Muselier, 22 March, 1941.

13   See Kemp, Paul: *Convoy! Drama in Arctic Waters*; London, Arms and Armour Press, 1993; pp. 132-134.

14   PRO ADM199/721. Reports of the Commanding Officers of ORP *Jastrazb*, HNorMS *St Albans* and HMS *Seagull*; pp. 99 *et seq*.

15   Hydrophone Effect

16   Roscoe, Theodore: *US Submarine Operations in World War II*; USNIP 1988; p. 418.

17   Rear Admiral Robert Welland's account dated 15 May, 1986. RNSM Archives.

18   Ibid.

19   Ibid.

*Chapter 7 (pp 93–107)*

1  DNC's *Submarine War Experiences*, Report of HMS *Sceptre*, Typescript copy in RNSM library.
2  Captain John Coote to Author, 17 May, 1989.
3  Commander Arthur Pitt to Author, 12 May, 1989.
4  Rear Admiral (Submarines, to CinC Home Fleet, 21 September 1939.
5  For a full account of Surcouf's short life see Richard Compton-Hall *Monsters and Midgets*, Blandford Press 1983 and James Rusbridger, *Who Sank Surcouf?*, Century Random House, 1991.
6  Imperial War Museum, Department of Photographs, correspondence with James Rusbridger, RUSB/J/PH.
7  Torpedoed on 30 June, 1942, by *U-372*.
8  RNSM *Thrasher* File: Ken Sunor to Jan Lock, 26 June 1989.
9  Vice Admiral Sir Hugh Mackenzie to Author, 7 February, 1989.
10  DNC's Submarine *War Experiences*, Report of HMS *Thrasher*, pp. 106-108. Typescript copy in RNSM library.
11  DNC's *Submarine War Experiences*, op. cit.
12  RNSM *Thrasher* File: Ken Sunor to Jan Lock, 26 June, 1989.
13  *Ibid, pp. 109-110.*
14  *Ibid, p. 109.*
15  Captain (S) One to CinC Med, August 1942.
16  Evans, A. S.: *Beneath the Waves*; London, William Kimber, 1986; pp. 327-8.

*Chapter 8 (pp 108–119)*

1  DNC's *Submarine War Experiences*: HMS *Sportsman* Patrol Report; Typescript copy in RNSM library.
2  *MAC* ships, Merchant Aircraft Carriers, were bulk grain carriers or oil tankers with the superstructure removed and fitted with a flight deck (some also had limited hangar facilities) for

operating four aircraft. They successfully combined the functions of merchant ship and aircraft carrier without detriment to either. Though the aircrew and supporting personnel were from the Royal Navy, the ships sailed under the Red Ensign and their officers and crew were from the Merchant Navy. Indeed some of their aircraft had Merchant Navy painted on their fuselage instead of the usual Royal Navy.

3   Cloarec's account of the last moments of *La Perle* is preserved in the French naval archives in Paris: file no. SHM TTY. 771.
4   Compton-Hall, Cdr Richard: *The Underwater War*; Blandford Books, 1982; p. 131.
5   PRO ADM. 199/1104, Report of Proceedings No. 3 June and July 1944,
6   HNethMS *Dolfijn* Patrol Report: Details supplied by the Institute of Maritime History, Royal Netherlands Navy.
7   Admiralty: Naval Staff History of the Second World War, *Submarines Vol III, Operations in Far Eastern Waters*; London, 1956; pp. 137-8.

## *Chapter 9 (pp 120–140)*

1   PRO ADM137/3745: Commodore British Adriatic Force (CCBAF) to Admiralty, 25 April 1918.
2   Simpson, Rear Admiral G. W.: *Periscope View, A Professional Autobiography*; London, Peter Davis, 1965.
3   SST: Supersonic Transmission – using the submarine's 129 Asdic set to transmit using morse code.
4   RNSM A1939/4: HMS *Oxley* Board of Enquiry, 23 September 1939.
5   Report of Proceedings of the Commanding Officer of HMS *Swordfish*, 21 September, 1939.
6   Report of Captain (S)2, 22 September, 1939.
7   Ibid.
8   RA(S) to CinC Home Fleet: 4 October, 1939.
9   PRO ADM 199/300.

10　PRO ADM 199/1837: Report of Proceedings of the Commanding Officer of HMS *Truant*.

11　PRO ADM 199/1837: op. cit. ,

12　PRO ADM 199/1837: Captain(S) 9th S/M Flotilla to VA(S), 5 August, 1940.

13　Ministry of Defence (Navy): *The U-boat War in the Atlantic 1939-1945*; London, HMS0, 1989; p. 68.

14　Op. cit. , p. 69.

15　Admiralty: *Monthly Anti-Submarine Report*; April 1943.

16　Ministry of Defence (Navy): *The U-boat War in the Atlantic, 1939-1945*; London, HMSO, 1989; p. 104.

17　PRO ADM236/48: Report of Proceedings of HM Submarine *Upholder*.

18　USS *Lapon: A Gato* class submarine built in 1942, displacing 2060/2424 tons and armed with ten 21" torpedo tubes (six bow, 2 stern) and a crew of 10 officers and 71 enlisted men.

19　USS *Lapon*, Patrol Report, US Submarine Force Library and Museum.

20　USS *Raton*, Patrol Report, US Submarine Force Library and Museum. The difference in time is due to the fact that *Raton* was keeping time one hour later than *Lapon*.

21　The submarine did not have to surface fully to use the 267 radar. It was possible to use the set while submerged by running with only the aerial, which was mounted on a fixed mast at the forward end of the periscope standards (the brackets supporting the periscopes above the conning tower), above the water.

22　Vice Admiral Sir John Roxburgh to author, 13 March 1989.

*Chapter 10 (pp 141–149)*

1　PRO ADM199/347 Comments of Captain(S)1 on *Tetrarch's* Patrol Report.

2　Cremer, Peter: *U-333 – the Story of a U-boat Ace*; Bodley Head,

1984; p. 43-45. Also patrol report of *U-333* from U-boot Archiv at Cuxhaven.

3 Herlin, Hans: *The Survivor – The True Story of the Sinking of the Doggerbank*; Leo Cooper, 1994.
4 Ufficio Storico della Marina Militare: La Marine Italiana Nella Seconda Guerra Mondiale, *Vol II; Navi Militare Perdute*; Rome 1975; p. 32.

## Chapter 11 (pp 150–163)

1 PRO ADM1/10560: Report of the Board of Enquiry into the loss of the French destroyer *Maille Breze*.
2 PRO ADM234/369, Admiralty: Naval Staff History of the Second World War, Battle Summary No. 22, *Arctic Convoys 1941-45*; London, 1954; p. 33.
3 Mk. XVIII torpedo: length, 20'5"; weight 3154lb; warhead, 575lb torpex; range 4,000 yards at 29 knots. The weapon was eventually discarded in 1950.
4 Roscoe, Theodore: *United States Submarine Operations in World War II; USNI*, Annapolis, 1949; p. 262.
5 O'Kane, Rear Admiral Richard: *Clear the Bridge! The War Patrols of the USS Tang*; Rand McNally, New York, 1977; p. 453.
6 O'Kane: op. cit. , p. 456.
7 For the record, the escape of the men from USS *Tang* was done from a depth greater than any had ever escaped from before using the Momsen Lung escape apparatus.
8 Fido: Mk. XXIV Anti Submarine Mine; length 84"; diameter 19"; weight 680lbs; warhead 92lbs Torpex; speed 12 knots.
9 Rear Admiral E. N. Poland to Author, 7 August, 1991.

*Chapter 12 (pp 164–175)*

1   Schwarzkopf, H. Norman: *It Doesn't Take A Hero*; New York, Bantam Press, 1992; p. 500.

2   Personal information supplied to the Author.

3   GPMG: General Purpose Machine Gun.

4   Woodward, Admiral Sir John: *One Hundred Days –The Memoirs of the Falklands Battle Group Commander*; London Harper Collins, 1992; p. 240.

5   1 Scots Guards, 1 Welsh Guards & 1/7 Gurkha Rifles together with support units.

6   Southby-Tailyour, Ewen: *Reasons in Writing – A Commando's View of the Falklands War*; London, Leo Cooper, 1993; pp. 265-266.

7   McManners, Hugh: The Scars of War; London, Harper Collins, 1993; p. 134.

8   Op. cit. , p. 134.

9   Southby-Tailyour: op. cit. , p. 272.

10   Commodore Amphibious Warfare.

11   Op. cit. , p. 273.

12   Eberlin, P.: *Underwater Acoustic Identification of Hospital Ships*; International Review of the Red Cross, November-December 1988; Geneva, ICRC, 1988.

12   Commander A. J. Pitt to Author, 12 May, 1989.

# Bibliography

Admiralty: *Führer's Conferences on Naval Affairs*; London; 1947.

Admiralty: Naval Staff History of the Second World War; Battle Summary No. 41, *The Evacuation of Dunkirk, Operation Dynamo, 26 May to 4 June, 1940*; London; 1949.

Admiralty: Naval Staff History of the Second World War; Battle Summary No. 47, *Okinawa-Operation Iceberg, March-June 1945*; London; 1950.

Admiralty: Naval Staff History of the Second World War, Battle Summary No. 22, *Arctic Convoys 1941-45*; London, 1954

Admiralty: Naval Staff History of the Second World War, Submarines Vol III, *Operations in Far Eastern Waters*; London, 1956; pp. 137-8.

Adams, T. A. & Lees D. J.: *Register of Type VII U-boats*; World Ship Society; 1991.

Alden, J. D.: *The Fleet Submarine in the US Navy*; USNI; 1979.

Allaway, J.: *Hero of the Upholder*; Airlife Books, 1993.

Bassett, Roland: *HMS Sheffield, The Life and Times of Old Shiny*: London, Arms and Armour Press; 1988.

Bickers R. T.: *Friendly Fire – Accidents in Battle from Ancient Greece to the Gulf War*; London, Leo Cooper; 1994.

Brice M.: *Axis Blockade Runners of WW2*; Blandford; 1981.

Brooke, Geoffrey: *Alarm Starboard; A Remarkable True Story of the War at Sea*; Patrick Stephens Ltd; 1982.

Brown, J. D.: *Warship Losses of World War II*; London, Arms and Armour Press; 1990.

Compton-Hall, Richard: *The Underwater War 1939-45*; Blandford; 1982.

Coote, John: *Submariner*; London, Leo Cooper; 1991.

Cremer, Peter: *U-333, The Story of a U-boat Ace*; London, Bodley Head; 1984.

English, J.: *The Hunts*; World Ship Society; 1987.

Evans A. S.: *Beneath the Waves*; London, William Kimber; 1986.

Fluckey, Eugene B: *Thunder Below!*; University of Illinois Press; 1992.

Gudgin P: *Tanks for the Memory – The Story of the 48th Battalion Royal Tank Regiment*; RTR Association; 1993.

Hill, Roger: *Destroyer Captain*; London, William Kimber; 1975.

Holmes, Harry: *The Last Patrol*; Airlife Books; 1994.

Kemp, Paul: *The T-Class Submarine*; London, Arms and Armour Press; 1990.

Kemp, Paul: *Convoy! Drama in Arctic Waters*: London, Arms and Armour Press; 1994.

Lange, Wilhelm: *Cap Arcona: Das Trägische Ende der KZ-Häftlings Flotte am 3. Mai 1945*; Struve's Buchdruckerei und Verlag, Eutin; 1988.

Lowe R. W. and Major J (Eds): *The Year of D-Day, The 1944 Diary of Admiral Sir Bertram Ramsay*; University of Hull Press; 1994.

McManners, Hugh: *The Scars of War*; London, Harper Collins, 1993.

Ministry of Defence: *The U-boat War in the Atlantic, 1939-45*; London, HMSO; 1989.

Montserrat, Nicholas: *The Cruel Sea*; London, Cassell; 1953.

Polmar N. & Carpenter D. B.: *Submarines of the Imperial Japanese Navy*; Conway Maritime Press; 1986.

Polmar N. & Noot J: *Submarines of the Russian and Soviet Navies, 1718-1990*; USNI; 1991.

Robertson, Terence: *The Ship with Two Captains*; London, Evans Brothers; 1957.

Roscoe, Theodore: *US Submarine Operations in WWII*; USNI; 1988.

Rusbridger J: *Who Sank Surcouf?*, London, Century Random House, 1991.

Simpson, Rear Admiral G. W.: *Periscope View: A Professional Autobiography*; London, Peter Davis; 1965.

Southby-Tailyour, Ewen: *Reasons in Writing – A Commando's View of the Falklands War*; London, Leo Cooper; 1993.

Stevens J. S.: *Never Volunteer – A Submariner's Scrapbook*; Solent Printers; 1971.

Ufficio Storico Della Marina Militare: *La Marina Italiana Nella Seconda Guerra Mondiale, Vol II, Navi Militari Perdute*; Rome 1975.

Williams, J. F.: *They Led the Way – The Fleet Minesweepers at Normandy*; J. Williams; 1994.

Whitley, M: *German Destroyers of World War Two*; London, Arms and Armour Press; 1983.

Woodman, Richard: *Arctic Convoys 1941-45*; London, John Murray; 1994.

Woodward, Admiral Sir John: *One Hundred Days – The Memoirs of the Falklands Battle Group Commander*; London, Harper Collins; 1992.

Young, Edward: *One of Our Submarines*; London, Hart Davis; 1954.

# Index

194

195

*Matabele*, HMS, destroyer, attacked by
HMS *Eskimo*, 26 Sept 1939, 26-27
*Max Schultz*, German destroyer, mined
22 Feb 1940, 41-42; investigation
into loss, 43-44
*MGB.87*, HMS, motor gun boat attacked
in error Apr 1942, 35
*MGB.89*, HMS, motor gun boat,
attacked in error Apr 1942, 35
*Minerve*, French submarine, 111
Mines, 160
Missile, problems associated with, 165
*ML-251*, HMS British motor launch,
sunk in error by HMS *Burdock*, 35-37
*Monarch*, cable layer, attacked by US
destroyers 13 Jun, 1944, 37-38
*Monte Gargano*, Italian depot ship, 65
*MTB.708*, HMS, damaged by
Beaufighters, 4 May, 1944, 52
*MTB-720*, HMS, damaged by
Beaufighters, 4 May, 1944, 52
*MTB-732*, HMS, attacked and sunk by FS
*La Combattante*, 27/28 May, 1944, 37

Napoleon, Emperor of France, 2
*Nairana*, HMS, escort carrier, 69
*Nankei Maru*, 162
Nash, Lieutenant Commander J,
commanding officer of HMS *Hussar*,
58, 59
Normandy, invasion of, 67

*0,21*, Dutch submarine, 79-81 passim
*0.23*, Dutch submarine, 79-81 passim
*O'Kane*, Lieutenant Commander (USN) R
H, commanding officer USS *Tang*,
154-7
*Otus*, HMS, British submarine, attacked by
HMS *Talisman* 8 Aug, 1941, 135-136
Owen, Lieutenant John, commanding
officer HMS *H-1*, 9
*Oxley*, HMS, British submarine, sunk by
HMS *Triton*, 122-124

*P-25*, HMS, patrol ship. 11-12
*P.514*, HMS, submarine, rammed and
sunk by HMCS *Georgian* 21 Jun,

1942, 84-85
Parham, Admiral Sir Frederick,
commanding officer of *P-25*, 11-12
*Pasley*, HMS, destroyer, sinks HMS *G-9*
19 Sept, 1917, 5-6
*Peter Hendriks*, rams and sinks HMS
*Umpire* Jul, 1941, 75-76
*Petunia*, HMS, corvette, 38
Pitt, Commander A, commanding officer
of HMS *Taku*, 94-95; on friendly fire,
175
*Plunkett*, US destroyer, attacks cable ship
*Monarch* 13 Jun, 1944, 38
*Pompano*, US submarine, 96
*Prabhavati*, RIN armed yacht, sunk by
HMS *Glasgow*, 8 Dec, 1944, 30–31
Price, telegraphist, J, in HMS *Britomart*,
57, 61-62, 64
*Prince of Wales*, HMS, British battleship,
65

Radar, 164-165
*Rakuyo Maru*, 162
Ramsay, Admiral Sir Bertram, on loss of
HMS *Britomart & Hussar*, 62
*Raton*, US submarine, 137-138
Recognition, marks carried by
submarines, 6-7, 15; problems of in
Adriatic 1917-18, 8-9; problems of
using periscopes, 9-10, ship
recognition, 13; aircraft recognition,
13, 40, 64-65; means of assuring, 14-
22 passim; challenge & reply system,
16-19, in Battle of Barents Sea, 24-26
Rivett-Carnac, Rear Admiral J W
(FOBAA), 62-63
*Rodney*, HMS, battleship, 65; in attack on
HMS *Trusty*, 87-90
Romanowski, Lieutenant Commander
Boris, in ORP *Jastrazb*, 82-84; in
ORP *Dzik*, 111
*Rorqual*, HMS, submarine, use of
pyrotechnic flares in, 18
*Rowell*, US destroyer, sinks USS *Seawolf*,
3 Oct, 1944, 85-87
*Rutherglen*, rams and sinks *H-5* 2 May,
1918, 6

196

197